MW00531727

THE AIRMAN BLUEPRINT
What You Need to Know to Excel in Today's Air Force

By
Brent Golembiewski

ISBN: 978-1-7354018-2-9 (eBook)
ISBN: 978-1-7354018-3-6 (Paperback)
ISBN: 978-1-7354018-4-3 (Audiobook)

1st Edition

For more information, e-mail: babajagapublishing@gmail.com

To my parents for giving me a firm foundation, my two boys and loving wife for the support and great times, and the Air Force for propelling me on an adventure of a lifetime.

For the brave men and women of the US Air Force both past, present, and future.

PREFACE

After recently retiring from twenty-plus years in the USAF, I reflected on my career—what I learned, what I could have done differently, and most importantly what I wish I had been taught by my superiors early in my career.

I have read plenty of leadership books, many of which are on the USAF "Read List," but I have found a topic missing. While all the leadership books tell you how to lead and how to be a good follower, none of them tell you what your leaders are looking for or what you need to do to excel in a rigid system like the USAF. In addition, there are some hidden rules I wish I had known about before taking my journey. With a bit of guidance on that, I could have avoided some of the pitfalls I encountered along the way.

This book, I hope, will fill that small void left out of most leadership books, courses, and mentor sessions. While this information on its own isn't groundbreaking, I will discuss multiple topics that are often misconstrued, poorly portrayed, and misunderstood from the perspective of a new or potential recruit.

In the interest of full disclosure, this book contains many of my own opinions, and as the saying goes, opinions are like (PC version) belly buttons: everyone has one. However, I will portray how I arrived at my particular opinions— and the advice I offer—by sharing the stories of my own Air Force experiences. Stories are one of the oldest learning techniques, and I believe we learn a lot by both sharing and hearing them.

I have done my best to tell you not only the good but the bad as well, because it wasn't always sunshine and rainbows, and I wish I had been better prepared for the swamps of sadness I sometimes felt. However, don't let my tales of bad times dissuade you in any way. In fact, I'd rather the opposite happen. My objective is for you to have the fullest extent of knowledge either before you join or as you begin your Air Force adventure. I recommend that every able-bodied person spend two years learning discipline and maturing in their own way through Air Force life. It gives you a great appreciation for those who gave us the rights we enjoy today.

This book is for anyone with an interest in the Air Force, both those currently serving in the Air Force and those deciding whether or not to join. Having been both enlisted and an officer, I will be going into detail about both sides of the equation. I've been a follower and a leader and have seen plenty of good and bad examples of each. I hope you find this information valuable as you continue along your path!

TABLE OF CONTENTS

CHAPTER ONE INTRODUCTION

How this book is laid out

I have laid out this book in a particular order to help you get the most out of it, retain what you read, and learn from my successes and failures. To that end, each chapter is part of an acronym: USAF AIRMAN. If you haven't yet been inundated with acronyms, you will be. The military loves them, and they can be a really effective way to remember key information.

Here is what each letter stands for—and what I'll cover in each chapter—in more detail:

U   **UNIFORM:** What is expected of you not only from your superiors but also society.

S   **STRENGTH:** This includes mental, physical, and emotional muscle.

A   **ADAPTABILITY:** How prepared are you for situations as they arise? Proper planning is key.

F   **FAMILY:** Maintaining the financial, emotional, and physical well-being of you and your family.

A   **ARTICULATION:** A fancy word for communication, a vital component of military and civilian life.

I   **IDENTITY:** This could be thought of as your personality, your character, your integrity and so on.

R   **RULES:** The Air Force is filled with them, and they range from black and white to shades of gray.

M   **MOTIVATION:** It's important to know the things that drive you to succeed.

A   **ADVANCEMENT:** This is not only your career progression but also how you mature personally.

N   **NATION:** See yourself as part of a team with the camaraderie that it brings.

Each chapter begins with a brief overview of its contents, as well as a few questions to ask yourself as you read through my stories, thoughts, and advice.

I'll end with a summary of what I learned about this topic and how you can effectively apply it as you move forward in the Air Force.

Back in my day . . .

Before we move on to the next chapter, I would like to share some of my backstory and of course my journey through the ranks of the United States Air Force.

I was born in Michigan to two awesome parents. My father was a machine repairman for General Motors—as blue-collar as they come. My mom was a schoolteacher who took time away from that career to raise both my younger sister and me.

After being constantly asked to join the Marines in high school, I was determined to *never* join the military.

In the summer of 1999, I attempted a semester of college, but I was torn between continuing my education, pursuing my dream of playing college hockey, and being with my girlfriend who was three hours away. I chose my girlfriend. She was my high school sweetheart, and it was a drain being away from her at college.

Looking back on it, a three-hour drive is nothing now that I have lived all over the country. I've spent six hours driving so that I could ski for two hours then turn around and drive another six hours back home.

Once I'd made the decision to drop out of college, I began to search for a job while living at home with my parents, who were less than thrilled with my decision. My girlfriend's dad helped me land a job at Sam's Club during the Christmas rush. I continued to work there after the holidays and was asked to stay on full-time.

Needless to say, it wasn't the most glamorous job, but I did my best. Eventually, the strain from living at home and trying to balance girlfriend time with work and family reached a boiling point. I had to do something.

So I headed to the place I'd never go: my local Air Force recruiting office. There I met a staff sergeant, and we started going over the process of enlisting and what I could expect from the Air Force. I received my physical, which if

you have already gone through it, felt like they made up the weirdest tests. While they didn't stick a needle in my arm and make it freak out like they did to the potential astronauts in the movie *The Right Stuff*, my exam seemed similar to the one in the film. Walking like a duck in my underwear was also a great time. (Just a little sarcasm there.)

After that fun was over, I took a written exam called the ASVAB (Armed Services Vocational Aptitude Battery). This test has multiple categories, including word knowledge, mathematics, mechanical aptitude, and many more. A few days later I was called to the recruiting office to go over the test and see what jobs I could choose from.

This is one nice thing about joining: you get to choose your job . . . sort of. After reviewing the test scores, I was informed I could get almost any job, but my highest scores were in Mechanical Comprehension (MC) and Electrical Information (EI).

Now here's the first little secret: recruiters really have no idea what tasks are done in the majority of Air Force jobs. Sure, they will know about a handful, but there are a multitude of career fields in the Air Force, and recruiters are only given a small paragraph to describe a job to you.

Today it is different, and they have better information to draw on, but if you are looking to join, then do your own homework and research online what jobs you are best qualified for. With the internet and so much information literally at your fingertips these days, a little research will go a long way and could help you land an incredibly awesome job.

In 1999, Google had only been invented less than a year prior and no one had heard of it yet, let alone a search engine for the "internet." There were no smartphones or Siri app to ask, "What does a [fill in the job title] do in the USAF?"

There was no awesome website with pictures and videos—just a few small sentences to learn about the job, talk the choice over with friends and family, and do some soul-searching into what drives you and what you would like to do. And yes, you will always be asked if you would like to be a cop (Security Forces in Air Force lingo). However, it's important to know that if you don't like your scores and the resulting job options, you can always retest.

As for me, because I had high marks in the mechanical section and the electronics section, I was allowed my pick of nearly any job in those categories. My recruiter showed me about ten that he thought sounded cool, but the one that caught my eye was Electronic Warfare Technician. In the job description it boasted that I'd be working on cutting-edge stealth technology. The recruiter and I read the paragraph explaining it:

> **"2A1x7 Electronic Warfare Technician:** *Technicians are responsible for maintaining and repairing USAF stealth equipment ensuring aircraft are undetected in the field of battle.*" (I later learned this is a huge paraphrase of the actual job.)

The recruiter, after reading it, added his own comments to reel me in: "I bet you work on the F-117 or B-2 stealth bombers."

Stealth technology? Awesome! I was hooked! And I got a $6,000 signing bonus—score— but had I done my research, I would have found out what that paragraph really meant. The job actually entailed maintenance on pods designed to jam enemy radar using transmitters on aircraft first utilized by the Wild Weasels in Vietnam. And as cool as that was, it was nowhere near as cool as the stealth fighter technology that I was led to believe I'd be working on.

I'm not saying the recruiter meant to lead me astray. He really just didn't know, and at the time, being young and naive, I didn't know how to do my own research. Had I looked up the information with my trusty 486 computer, I may have been able to find the real tech I'd be working on, but these were the days of chat rooms and AOL. (Look it up; I'm not giving you what AOL stands for.)

A week later, I headed to MEPS (Military Entrance Processing Station), where they did some final tests. Somewhere along the way I was sworn in and stayed at a hotel that night. (I guess they didn't want their new catch to run.)

I flew out of Detroit to San Antonio the next morning and rode a bus to Lackland AFB, where I was greeted by a nice man yelling at the top of his lungs, very much reminding me of Gunnery Sergeant Hartman in the film *Full Metal Jacket*.

It was here at basic training that I received my first shocking misunderstanding. When my first paycheck arrived, I was pretty excited but when I opened it up—WHAT? You may hear that the military supplies you with everything from food to uniforms, boots, etc. Well, they do, but they deduct those costs from your paycheck during basic. I was caught off guard, but I was fine since I had no bills at the time. No bills—that's funny. It seems like a dream now.

After basic training and tech school, I found myself at Shaw AFB working on the tried-and-true AN/ALQ-184 jamming pod. After some time, two airmen who were overseeing my on-the-job training took me under their wings and introduced me to a commissioning program called OTS (Officer Training School).

I'd had one semester of college and vowed I'd never go back. Remember what I said about joining the military in high school? I'm sensing a theme here. These two senior airmen were attending night school and applying to become officers, and while that sounded cool in its own right, the pay sounded even better. If you're reading this online, go ahead and check it out with this link. I'll wait.

https://www.dfas.mil/militarymembers/payentitlements/Pay-Tables.html

They laid out the yellow brick road for me to follow, and it seemed like a can't-miss opportunity. I began taking class after class as my education counselor suggested. I really didn't care which classes I took; I was just looking to get through it as quickly and as painlessly as possible. The funniest part was that these classes would have helped me later in my career had I actually paid attention . . .

I was taking four classes a semester when I found out about a program called Bootstrap, now called the Air Force Educational Leave of Absence (AFELA) Program. This fantastic program allows someone who is one semester from graduating to go to school full-time, not work, and still get paid. This was a fantastic way to finish my degree. I took eight classes in my last semester and was able to finish my bachelor's degree just about one year after I started.

Here's a tidbit of knowledge: The Air Force and all the other services have a plethora of these types of programs. What's more, they paid for 75 percent of my school, and I used my MGI Bill to pay the other 25 percent. Want free school? Doesn't get much better than that, and we haven't even gotten to my main points yet!

Back to the story at hand. During my school push, I was also working hard at my job. Because I listened to the more experienced members around me and absorbed as much as I could, I found myself being asked to work on malfunctioning ECM Pods that most others couldn't figure out. Now I'm not saying I'm a genius—far from it. I'm Polish, come on. But I asked questions and studied the systems, going above and beyond what most of my peers did.

The joke about avionics techs was that we were just card pullers. The avionics would malfunction, then we would look up the culprit circuit board and remove and replace it. This was how 90 percent of the troubleshooting was done, simple and pretty effective. However, we also went through six months of avionics school, which teaches basic electronics.

While most of my peers dumped this knowledge or just didn't continue to expand upon it, I did. This helped me to use my own knowledge and lean on the knowledge of more experienced technicians to repair equipment that the majority of the shop couldn't. Unintentionally, I began to stand out, and I soon found myself on a special team to test the Radar Warning Receiver (RWR) systems on our F-16s.

This became a high-visibility job, and I soon found myself briefing generals on our capabilities, findings, and fixes of the malfunctioning systems. I really didn't like public speaking and still don't, but my sergeants saw my drive and pushed me into the role.

What I got out of it was a letter of recommendation for officer training school from the wing commander (the highest-ranking officer on the base). This greatly increased the chances of my acceptance to the school with my package submittal. I began Bootstrap, and with that golden ticket, I applied to Officer Training School.

Applying for OTS meant filling out a book of paperwork, including my list of job preferences, a.k.a. my dream sheet. After plenty of thought, I decided I wanted new challenges, so I put down my three choices. Nothing glamorous. I just wanted to become an officer.

A short time after submitting my package, I was ordered to report to my commander. I thought, *Crap, what did I do?* I had plenty of thoughts going through my head when I arrived at the commander's office, reported in, and was told to have a seat. My commander then told me he wanted to discuss my OTS package. He was a very good commander, knew everyone by their first name, and seemed genuinely interested in everyone's work when he would visit our shop.

He began with, "I see your preferences are . . ." and he listed off the choices I had made. *Oh, no!* I thought. *Is he going to ask me why I didn't put Maintenance on it?* Instead, he went in a different direction, one I was not expecting. He raised one of his hands to just below chest level and said, "This is where officers are." He then raised his other hand to eye level and stated, "This is where pilots are. I believe you would make an excellent pilot, and I think you should change your job choices." I thanked him for his glowing endorsement of my abilities and left.

I gave it some serious thought. Images of Tom Cruise shooting down MiGs flew through my head. After discussing it with my family, I decided to put "Pilot" on my application. Now, I didn't have a single flight hour. In fact, I think I may have been on two flights before my plane ride to San Antonio for basic training.

The buzzkill was I had to write an essay as to why I wanted to be a pilot. This almost made me give up. (Silly, I know.) I hated writing and had no idea where to start, but with the help of a very good friend, I completed the essay and submitted it with my package.

A few short weeks before I was to finish my degree, I was called into the shop. My commander was there and passed on the great news I had been selected for OTS. Excited at this success, I didn't even think about what my job was going to be until someone asked me. The paper said 92TO. What the heck did that mean? I was told to go to the education office so they could decipher it.

When I handed the paper to the woman at the education office, the first words out of her mouth were "92TO—hmm, I've never seen that before." Just what I wanted to hear. What the heck had I gotten myself into? She then flipped through some pages of a book and stopped at a page while I eagerly and fearfully waited for her to read the job title. "Oh, it says Student Pilot," she announced. I was in shock, couldn't believe it, and sat there dumbfounded for a few minutes before leaving.

With my career path now laid out before me, I finished my degree through Embry-Riddle and was off to Officer Training School. Remember those classes I mentioned earlier that would have come in handy had I paid attention? Have you guessed what they were yet? They were aerodynamics classes. Funny how things work out.

After graduating from OTS, I was then sent to Columbus, Mississippi, one of three pilot training bases. Through a program at the time, the Air Force paid me to attend a civilian pilot school, and I received my private pilot's license flying a Cessna 152 at the local FBO (Fixed Base Operator) at an airport near the base.

Next, it was on to UPT Phase One (Undergraduate Pilot Training), where after an intense ground school, I began flying the T-37 "Tweet," as it was affectionately called due to its high-pitched almost useless turbine engines. During this phase of training, I was again confronted with many challenges.

I quickly learned that fighter pilots were not cool athletes as portrayed in the movie *Top Gun*, but nerds. They were all nerds. Well-adjusted nerds, but nerds nonetheless. Pilot training required a lot of attention to detail, memorization, and book smarts. Needless to say, I struggled but continued to improve.

However, I realized how much I didn't know yet when during the first phase of flight I struggled with the straight-in approach to landing. Now, all of you pilots out there are probably saying, "Man, that's one of the easiest landings." Well, not for me with only fifty hours of flight time to that point. I struggled enough that I was allowed a couple of extra runs before my check ride—the pilot's test.

The seating configuration in the Tweet was side-by-side, unlike most fighter aircraft which are front and back or tandem. It was during my first extra flight while shooting the approach that out of the corner of my eye I saw my instructor contort and twist his upper body so he could look at me.

He just sat there staring at me while I frantically manipulated the controls. I tried all I could to fly the approach. Finally, he said, "Do you really want to be a pilot?" I was crushed but I was determined to become better. A ride or two after that I made it through Phase I and continued training.

In pilot training they organize you into classes, then once you hit the "flight line" or flying phase, they split the class into two flights. Each flight had about eight instructors who would join you in the plane. You stayed with your flight, and those were the only eight instructors you would fly with.

Out of the two flights, my half got the tough instructors—and, no, I'm not just saying that. Our sister flight admitted as much. This was mainly because the flight commander was a crusty, old passed-over major, and his disgruntled attitude filtered down to the other instructors.

As time went on, I realized I wanted to fly helicopters, which back then were considered the red-headed stepchild of aircraft. Luckily, my ground school grades and flight grades were good enough for me to have my choice. My classmates were very excited that I wanted helicopters because none of them did, and it all worked out as I was the only one in the class to actually get a helicopter.

After successfully completing the first half of pilot training, I was moved to Fort Rucker, Alabama, to learn to fly the UH-1H Huey helicopter. This meant more ground school and learning to fly all over again. Helicopters fly like airplanes once you're moving forward, but there was the whole hover thing. No auto hover in the Huey—it was all hands.

I quickly realized this was my calling. Something about helicopters seemed almost easier. I have since changed back to flying planes, and they actually are way easier to fly, but I enjoyed flying helicopters, and the enjoyment helped me improve overall. I was able to study better and felt more comfortable flying.

Don't get me wrong—it was very stressful and very challenging, but something about having a better understanding of aviation along with struggling through fixed-wing training helped me excel.

As a result, I was given the present of a Huey and assignment in Minot, North Dakota. I was off to the "great white north" of the United States, or so I thought. I soon learned all the North Dakota snow blows into Minnesota. There's also a pretty girl behind every tree, and it's the only state where it's so flat you can see your dog running away for three days before it disappears.

Once in North Dakota, I felt like I had finally arrived as a full-fledged pilot. No more flight training. I learned my job as a copilot as well as my "additional duties," a term that for most becomes synonymous with "primary duties."

My initial extra duty was putting publications in aircraft and handling some of the paperwork for unit check rides. After some issues (more on these later), I attended aircraft commander school at Kirkland, progressed less than a year later to Instructor School, and then headed back to Minot.

Shortly after returning from Instructor School, I had my very first "in-house" student. I failed miserably that day as an instructor because I thought my student had already had a flight or two in the unit. It turned out that instruction flight was her first flight, and I was supposed to teach her all the items that I scolded her about not knowing. Though my initial impression was not good, to say the least, she would later marry me. As I said earlier, funny how things turn out.

On completing my four years at Minot and turning around my work habits, I was rewarded with a move to Fairchild AFB in Spokane, Washington. There I became a member of the Thirty-Sixth Rescue Flight and began to excel in flying.

As a result of honing my skills as a helicopter pilot and spending one year in Iraq, I was again rewarded by my commander selecting me to attend the Canadian Helicopter Course in Penticton, Canada. This course taught me advanced flying skills and opened my eyes to new ways of flying, many of which have now been adopted in the USAF helicopter community.

After my time in Spokane, I was sent to Andrews AFB near Washington, DC, and began working at the First Heli. Upon learning the mission and becoming fully qualified, I worked to help bring what I learned at previous assignments to the younger pilots at Andrews.

Then it was off to F .E. Warren AFB in Cheyenne, Wyoming. I arrived there just as a new helicopter group was being created and aircraft-mounted weapons were being added to our Hueys. I learned and taught the new systems as together we brought additional innovative capabilities to the USAF.

I retired from the Air Force in 2019 and have begun pursuing other opportunities in flying.

Okay, I know that was a lengthy introduction, but I wanted to give you the CliffsNotes on my USAF career as I will pull from these and other stories to explain my points in the coming chapters.

Now on to the good stuff.

CHAPTER TWO: UNIFORM

Uniform - *remaining the same in all cases and at all times; unchanging in form or character.*
["blocks of stone of uniform size" – Oxford English Dictionary]

This chapter covers what it means to put on the uniform, to have people watching your every step when in either the physical USAF uniform or in civilian attire. You can never hide from the public no matter how much you think you're blending in. In addition, it is a great honor to serve. Not everyone can do it, and by putting on the uniform, you become part of a select group capable of outstanding achievements.

As you read through my stories, ask yourself these questions and see if you can glean the same knowledge I learned.

Questions to ask yourself:

- Question 1: Why am I serving or why do I want to serve?
- Question 2: How do my actions affect the civilian population's view of Air Force members?
- Question 3: What can I do to stay up to USAF standards?

USAF core values

There are three core values you will learn in the Air Force:
- Integrity First
- Service Before Self
- Excellence in All We Do

Together, these form the cornerstone of how you should conduct yourself, and they are drilled into your core being. While some older USAF members may roll their eyes over these (I know I once did), there is a lot to be said for all three. They do ring true, and they each need to be looked at individually.

Integrity First

Let's start with integrity. I have seen firsthand how people have lost their integrity. It led them down a dark path, eventually landing them in Leavenworth (a military prison for those who don't know).
When I was at Minot AFB, a high-speed security forces member was working very hard and had been flying with us on the Tactical Response Force (TRF) for a few years. This assignment wasn't given just to any security forces member. At the time, it was a select group chosen for their hard work and their tactical skill. In addition to the normal instruction, they would be sent to assault school, sniper school, and other additional trainings.

This individual was doing very well and was one of the best we had. He worked well with the crew and knew his tactics for guiding other teams to victory during exercises. In his spare time, he was working on his bachelor's degree and was going to apply to officer training school, a similar path as my own, so I fully supported him.

After completing his degree, he submitted the package and shortly afterwards was accepted. I thought it was great and that it was turning out to be an amazing journey for the young man. Weeks went by, and I noticed he hadn't flown with us, so I asked where he was. Turns out he was caught selling Night Vision Goggles (NVGs) on eBay.

I was dumbfounded. Obviously, his OTS slot was taken from him, and he ended up in Leavenworth, a far cry from being an officer—and for what? A few hundred dollars? Integrity will save you if you let it.

Service Before Self

That brings me to our second core value: service before self. In my opinion, everyone generally finds this difficult, probably because people are selfish. I know I probably offended a good number of you, but if you don't think so, read the hundreds if not thousands of books on the subject.

What do you do in a conversation if it's stalling? Get the person talking about themselves; nine out of ten will go on and on with no end in sight. Have you noticed how plenty of people are just waiting for their turn

to speak? It's because they want to talk about themselves or they want accolades about their opinion. While this is a generality, it's what makes the second core value the hardest to keep.

Placing yourself before your work can have ramifications beyond yourself. An example is putting off paperwork. I've endured the repercussions of this plenty of times. I would be on leave and get a message saying, "I just got your performance report done. Can you come in on leave and sign it so we won't break the deadline?" Yes, that happened to me, not once but three times . . . in a row.

All of us have some desire to serve a greater good, and that's a part of why we join. However, that might not be the driving force behind our actions, and we need to remember to take a step back and see how our actions will affect the Air Force as a whole. On the flip side, service before self can be an emotional uplift. There is something about working hard and helping the team succeed that is fulfilling and propels you forward.

I have stayed late or worked long hours during deployments and exercises to accomplish a goal not for myself but for the team. When we do that, we get to see others succeed—and that can be as enjoyable as you being the one to succeed.

As a pilot we typically become instructors. Watching a student struggle, giving them a little more knowledge, maybe working with them more than you have "time" for, watching them succeed, and eventually seeing them go on to be an instructor themselves is motivating. So when you're at the office late launching that aircraft at hour eleven of your day, know that it's worth it. It is what makes us the greatest Air Force in the world.

Excellence in All We Do

This one is a bit easier for most. We all want to be good at our jobs. Very few people wake up in the morning, turn off their alarm clock, and say, "Hey, I suck at my job, and I think I'll just continue to suck today." It doesn't work that way. As human beings we want to excel, but sometimes things are difficult.

When I was in Iraq, my Iraqi counterpart had a saying he would recite when we were starting a new, challenging project: "step by step." Simple, right? As a motivator, it's easy to remember, and it is so true. You can't excel at anything if you don't take the first step, and if you try to skip that first step (or any steps), you'll fall flat on your face. The next time you face a huge challenge, remember to take the first step, and everything else will follow along.

Remember your core values, tweak them to be yours, and you will have a great Air Force career.

When is it time to get a haircut?

This was asked of my Officer Training School class one day by our instructor. One trainee said when it's out of regulations, another said every week. This went on for about five to ten minutes with no one giving the answer our instructor was looking for.

As an Air Force member, you are held to all sorts of standards, but the important one that applies to everyone, whether mechanic, personnel troop, or pilot, is the *Air Force Instruction 36-2903: Dress and Appearance.*

If you don't have the number memorized yet, you will. It will be referenced more than any other single regulation throughout your entire career. While it is constantly changing, the majority of it has withstood the test of time and hasn't drastically changed much.

Two of the hot topics for the majority of members have to do with hair, both facial and on your head. I'm going to mainly speak to the male side, but this also applies to the females as well. The answer to the above question is never. I know you're saying, "Wait, you have to be in regulations, and you need a haircut to do that." While all that is true, the point is that you should always be in regulations, so technically you don't ever need a haircut.

This applies to so many things in general because there is always someone watching you and taking notice. It's truly a small world, and you may be out to dinner at a local restaurant when who walks in but your commander. While you may not get downgraded on your performance

report for being a little out of regulations, he/she is taking notice. We all are human, and (news flash) there is no way to eliminate bias, but if you look and act the part of an airman, there will be no issues.

Fun fact: The Air Force is always trying to eliminate biases. In the past, for example, a picture had to be included in promotion packages. It was changed to prevent the bias that attractive people who "looked" like senior ranking officers or enlisted would be chosen over other individuals who had higher marks, were harder workers, or were flat-out better at their jobs than their peers.

After removing the picture requirement, however, other things took its place, and there is still bias regardless of what anyone says. In short, you will be judged on your appearance, and looking the part will help you excel.

Oh, say, can you see

We stood at parade rest awaiting the national anthem. It was the first day of Flickerball (more on that later), and all four squadrons were gathered on the parade field ready to start this new challenge. We all came to attention, and the national anthem played. Not much different than any other small opening ceremony I had attended. This was only Squadron Officer School (SOS) anyway, nothing like a big NFL game.

The national anthem came to a close with the sound of jet engines. It seemed they were getting louder. Not thinking too much of it, I looked to see what was going on along with all the other students. To my surprise a big black wing was nearly on top of us, at about two thousand feet would have been my guess. A B2 bomber! For a Flickerball game? You bet. I was amazed, and it definitely gave me the feels, as you might say.

Being part of the greatest Air Force ever has its perks. While the hours are long, grueling, and plenty of times thankless, times like that make it worth it. I had been to plenty of air shows and had never seen the B2 fly over at normal height, let alone so close.

Working on or with the people who maintain, manage, and fly some of the most sophisticated aircraft in the world is a great experience. Yet there will be

times when you'll wonder why you joined. Everything loses its luster at times. I have known plenty of people, including myself, who have gone through some tough times when the Air Force seemed like the worst place to work, but then something like that B2 happens, or you have a civilian thank you for your service. At first you might just shrug it off, but you have earned this. Even if you are not on the front lines turning wrenches or flying aircraft, you are an integral piece of the puzzle, and the Air Force would fold without you.

Having managed multiple people, I can tell you firsthand how difficult it is to try and do things by yourself or with less-than-stellar teammates. The better and more professional you are, the better everyone else will be. That simple flyover reminded me of one of the reasons why I joined the Air Force, and it helped "re-blue" me, as they say.

As you journey through your Air Force career, you will have some ups and downs. Always remember the big picture and find a way to keep reminding yourself of it.

G's lessons learned

So you've finished chapter 2, which was pretty short and sweet. Now on to the summary.

We all join for a variety of reasons, but in the end, there is, at least for the majority of us, a sense of duty, honor, and love of country. Being part of something bigger than yourself is an amazing motivating factor, and knowing that everyone is always watching you can be a big pressure cooker, but it's still worth it.

You will have many choices throughout your career, and your character will play a big role in it. Set the foundation early. While you may slightly modify your preferences, as I did, remember throughout your career that you are part of a greater culture, and your actions speak to the world. People will be watching you all the time. Remember that, and it will help you navigate life in the Air Force.

The standards and rules are there for a reason, and following them will help keep you on a path for greatness. If you don't understand them or think they don't apply, seek guidance and clarification.

There will always be someone who has already accomplished what you are setting your sights on, so find them and utilize their knowledge.

CHAPTER THREE: STRENGTH

Strength - *the capacity of an object or substance to withstand great force or pressure.*

This chapter covers not only your physical strength and abilities but also your mental toughness. Both are essential for today's airman. You will sometimes work long hours in stressful environments, and these are keys to your success.

Questions to ask yourself:

- Question 1: How do you prepare yourself for a challenge?
- Question 2: Do you give up easily or push through barriers?
- Question 3: What can you do to become stronger both physically and mentally?

The big, bad word: FITNESS

At the time of this writing, each Air Force member has four fitness events to accomplish, if you call the waist measurement an event. They are the 1.5-mile run, which is based on time and feels more like a sprint than a distance run; pushups; sit-ups; and the waist measurement. Each service is different, and they are constantly changing them.

Every physical testing (PT) system has flaws, and when I came in the Air Force, I had to take the almighty bike test. You would have wires hooked up to you, sit on a stationary bike, and begin pedaling. The machine would take your baseline heart rate, then the examiner would increase the tension on the bike until your heart rate would rise. They would continue to add a little tension until your heart rate would rise into the testing zone.

For individuals who had low resting heart rates, a lot more tension had to be added, which then caused their heart rates to spike. Some good, in-shape athletes would fail the test because of this. I failed the bike test once, and not because I was in stellar shape. I was actually fat, and I have added a picture of my fat phase.

Before I tell you my story, let me get into what the Air Force wants and why they keep changing this system. They want the picturesque, in-shape individual (not the round type) who is healthy and also good-looking.

The problem is that there is no way to test for all the things they want. If you just want skinny runners, then, sure, the one-and-a-half-mile run is great. If you want someone who can carry a wounded airman off the battlefield, then the run doesn't matter so much. It's the strength tests that would matter.

Then there is the male-versus-female scale. I understand what they are going for: overall health. While there are outliers, women are not as fast or as strong on average as men, except in the sit-up; they are amazing at that one. The Air Force changes the scales to account for gender differences. If this was totally skills-based, the system would be the same for both genders.

However, until the Air Force has different tests for different body types, the system will be flawed. For example, there should be one fitness test for athletes (think larger guys, academy football players); one for runners (I know a guy who only runs once a year for the PT test and scores one hundred); and one for your average person who's well-rounded.

In my opinion, the best thing would be to just have the test as part of your yearly physical and incorporate the bod pod. For those of you who don't know what it is, you should try it. It's this big pod or bubble (think cryogenic chamber on any sci-fi movie) that you climb into to test your body fat percentage. Combined with heart rate and blood work, this is one of the best ways to test an individual's health, and it would accomplish the Air Force's goal of easily identifying healthy individuals. The only risk would be people getting labeled as fat, or the PC term, obese.

I have always been frustrated with the PT test, and not because I had to test, but mainly with how heavily it is weighed on the one-and-a-half-mile run. While I hate tests, and especially running because it's horrible on your knees, I want to excel in any physical activity. It is just in my nature to be competitive in an event such as the PT test.

While I was deployed to Iraq, I thought it would be prime time to achieve that elusive perfect PT score. I had recently been placing around ninety-two out of one hundred in the last few PT tests but wanted to try to achieve one hundred. For most people, anything above ninety was a win due to the fact that only one PT test was due each year. If you scored below ninety but still passed, you had six months until your next test. I won't even go into what happens if you fail. Best to avoid that!

To train for my perfect score, I worked out differently, incorporating more cardio and more running than I wanted to do. Then test day came. That day I was the only one testing, so after performing the pushups, the sit-ups, and waist measurement, we headed out to the makeshift track on the flight line.

On a side note, when possible, request the reverse PT test where you run first then accomplish the pushups and sit-ups. I have done it that way with better results and less effort.

The track was three-quarters of a mile out then three-quarters of a mile back. I lined up and headed out on the command "go." I felt like I was making a good pace and continued to keep up the speed as best I could. I reached the return line, was halfway there, and I felt good. I found myself trying to quicken the pace but had topped out and didn't want to use everything up before the final sprint.

Near the end I could hear my tester shouting out the numbers, which at the time meant nothing to me. I gave it all I had, attempting to make the best possible time. I crossed the finish, heard some numbers given to me, then walked it off. I eagerly awaited my score after catching my breath. I was less than five seconds short and received a ninety-nine on the test. It was that day I determined the test wasn't built for healthy athletes but for runners. I resigned myself to that fact and concentrated on my health instead of putting the extra wear and tear on my knees.

I continued to score in the nineties for the rest of my career, ensuring I only had to run once a year. You only get one body, no upgrading to a newer model, so make sure you take care of it.

In the end you need to stay in shape for yourself. My officer career started with none of that in mind. Let me tell you my story, then I'll go into my overall thoughts on PT and the Air Force. If you look at my pictures now, I am in decent shape, I work out five times a week, and I have broken the myth of retirement fat. Here's to you doubters who all said I would get fat when I retired. But I wasn't always this way.

If you remember in my introduction, I mentioned I grew up playing sports. But unlike today where the term "gym rat" is thrown around, back in the 1990s there wasn't a premium on the gym. Unless you were

a bodybuilder, you typically would spend little time in the gym working more on overall fitness and more on muscle building.

I often wonder if this is partially why athletes are so fragile these days. There is some truth to the quote, "A gime, what's a gime?"

For all the sports I played, we practiced all the time on the field or ice but never frequented the gym. Even my football team didn't lift weights much, unless you were a lineman. Maybe that's why we never won a game in high school. My memories of the gym are random weights lying around, Metallica's "King Nothing" playing on a constant loop, and big linemen bench pressing. Needless to say, I really didn't know my way around the gym.

While I was enlisted, I played softball on the squadron team and generally kept myself in what I thought was decent shape. Then pilot training hit, and I realized I was a mess when it came to my body. Between the constant studying, eating out literally every meal, little to no sleep, and laying on the couch when I did have time, I ballooned to 205 pounds. And I'm not talking about NFL wide receiver 205. I was fat.

I failed the bike test, which was the first scare, but a dunk test proved my fat was still in the healthy range, and I was able to pass that way. It was a little embarrassing, but I was still in pilot training and that was my focus. After making it through pilot training, I arrived at my first duty station in Minot, North Dakota. Yes, I did watch *Fargo* before we moved there, which was a big mistake.

Then my first wife got antsy and left for California. Now that is another whole story, so let's stick with fitness. Suddenly I had a lot of time on my hands. I found the gym. I bought fitness magazines, looked up workouts online, and loved it! Where had this been all my life? Oh yeah, it was always there but never a priority. If you're interested in additional reading, I would recommend *The Miracle Morning* by Hal Elrod. It details a morning process that successful people follow, and one of the most important steps is fitness.

After finding the gym, I continued to still play softball, flag football, and anything else I could do outside, but the gym was a revelation. Maybe it

was the cold winters or knowing that I had to get into the dating game that pushed me there, but that's not the case. Being a helicopter pilot at Minot in the early 2000s meant I was flying my tail off, literally.

I had arrived as the sole copilot, and it would be months before the next one arrived. What did that mean? It meant that they would throw me on any scheduled flight. At first, I loved it, but it took a toll on me. I upgraded to aircraft commander and the same thing occurred. The Flight was short on aircraft commanders, so I flew all the time.

It was at this time my lower back started hurting a bunch. I went to the flight doc, and while they were great in the sense that, short of losing a limb, they would clear you to fly, I was told my back was weak and given Motrin, or vitamin M, as we referred to it. This didn't help the situation, and I continued flying a lot.

Finally, after a few more trips to the flight doc and physical therapy, I was in no better shape, so I made one more attempt at the flight doc. I arrived at the office like I had the previous times but had done some research for this appointment. I had a secret weapon, one that had to work. It was one word, actually an acronym.

They ushered me back to the exam room, and I slowly made my way hunched over like an old man. It was the previous day's flight that made me finally go back to the flight doc. By now, our squadron was short on pilots, so I was trying to be the best teammate, suck it up, and fly.

That flight I hobbled out to the aircraft and climbed into the seat like Father Time had caught up to me. My back hurt so much I couldn't use the pedals. And for a helicopter pilot this is a bad thing, a very bad thing. I told my copilot he would be flying the whole sortie and that he'd better have his "A-Game," because if we had any malfunctions, I would be of little use. After landing, I had decided that flying that way was anything but safe, and while I trusted my copilot, I needed to get this fixed.

So there I was, waiting for the doctor in the exam room. Finally, the door opened and it was the doc we affectionately called Doogie for his resemblance to Doogie Howser. Look it up. It used to be a TV show about a kid doctor.

He greeted me, looked over my records, and asked how bad the pain was.

"Would it be possible to get an MRI?" I responded. Shots across the bow. I have a few doctor friends and I know it frustrates them when their patient thinks they know what's wrong, but I was to a point where I felt insane doing the same thing over and over with no results.

Doogie looked at me and said, "I think it's time to get you an MRI."

Now, in my head I was thinking, *About time!* But I just smiled and said thank you.

The MRI went at military high speed: it only took two weeks to get an appointment, then another two weeks to get the diagnosis. I was called in for my follow-up appointment and sat in the exam room awaiting the doctor. Once again, Doogie popped in. As much as I wanted to be healthy, I was hoping they found something minor that would explain my troubles. "Looks like you have a bulging disc and a minor herniated disc between your S1 and L5," Doogie stated.

For those of you non doctors out there, it meant the soft pad between my tailbone and the first vertebrae in my back was squished (yes, technical term), and the filling was leaking. Think of a jelly-filled donut with the filling oozing out. This was not a good thing, but luckily it wasn't bad enough to create shooting pains down my legs.

I was given more physical therapy and more Motrin, but with this new diagnosis my health goals changed. I decided it was time to get in shape. As I was writing this the theme to the movie *Rocky* popped into my head, but it wasn't quite like that. I slowly started working out. I bought magazines, started experimenting with supplements, and eventually fell in love with the gym. After a few months, I was seeing results, then after about a year, I was down to 185 pounds and in good shape.

Then something amazing happened, and everything was easier, physically speaking. Not having that added weight made me feel healthier, more confident. The helicopter preflight, walking, playing sports, everything—better! The only downside was that winter was cold! In Minot it would get to thirty below zero. In my fat phase I

would wear a flight suit and thermals; now it was flight suit, thermals, and a heavy winter flight jacket.

Sometimes I would even break out my "astronaut" gloves, so named by myself because anytime I wore them, I was tempted to touch switches in the cockpit in super slow motion like you see in *Apollo 13*. They were very thick heavy gloves.

As time moved along, I spent a year in Iraq and continued to experiment with exercises and supplements. I finally found that my body works best on regular food and settled on taking a caffeine pre-workout supplement since I don't drink coffee or tea. I have since removed the caffeine and have found the results to be much better than when I was on the "juice."

What I want you to take away from this is that everyone is different. You may like yoga, or biking, or even the dreaded running, but if you commit to doing some sort of physical activity to keep your body functioning correctly, life will be easier. I see many of my friends struggling with different things and a lot of the symptoms come from weight gain.

We are very blessed to be in the United States, and we have many comforts, some of which contribute to ongoing weight gain. Two examples include eating fast food and overly processed meals. Any self-help book can lead you down the path of healthy eating and exercise, and I'm preaching that same message.

One great thing about the Air Force is that part of your job is to be healthy. Depending on your squadron, you may do unit PT, but I find this inadequate. Take the time to work out on your own. Ask your supervisor if you can have time at the gym. Most commanders will give you additional time on top of your lunch time to work out. I remember as far back as when I was enlisted that guys would take two-hour lunches, spending one hour of it in the gym. But don't abuse this, actually use it.

Know that the food side will be the toughest part. While the Air Force preaches fitness, there are plenty of what I call "Diet Destroyers." For example, the last base where I was stationed just had a Dunkin' Donuts added on base. If that isn't anti-health food, I don't know what is. In

addition, many of my units had a tradition to bring donuts for your penance if you were late.

We are social animals, and where do we gather? Lunch, parties, BBQs, all with some horrible food choices. You will have to execute some willpower or bring your own snacks. To sum it up, you only get one body—take care of it!

The Middle East vs the West

What I learned about the Air Force and the culture of the Middle East shaped the whole second half of my career and changed the way I thought about world issues. I have never been one to watch the news. In fact, I had a friend tell me it was almost un-American to not watch the news.

I've always had the attitude that since I can't change things, so why bring all that negativity into my life. But when I found myself deploying to Iraq, I paid more attention. I wanted to better understand the people and culture I would be dealing with on a day-in-day-out basis.

I was sent to Fort Dix for advisor school and learned about elements of Middle Eastern culture, such as their traditions, customs, holidays, and beliefs. At the same time, I also learned tactical convoy driving, including armored vehicles, small-arms training, and hand-to-hand fighting techniques. One main point that was driven home throughout the training was that because the culture was vastly different than ours, we needed to help them develop their Iraqi way and not try to change them into Americans.

My job when I arrived was to advise the Iraqi Air Force how to train, fight, and win like us. Do you see the contradiction already? My title was Iraqi Air Force Helicopter Operations Advisor. My mission was to advise my Iraqi counterparts on what to do as they rebuilt their air force.

As soon as I arrived and completed the handoff with the captain I was replacing, I realized a lot of the training we received had not made it into the country—namely, with the top brass. As Westerners we are goal-oriented and want measurable success. Every week there were mandatory briefings on how many pilots we trained, how much infrastructure we

had built, and how the logistics plans were coming along—all tangible, measurable goals so we could wipe our hands clean and go home.

However, the Iraqis didn't follow numbers; they would figure things out their own way. Tracking programs were in place only on our side. They would leave at any moment, or not show up for months.

One day while executing my third different job down in Basra, we had scheduled a class for a number of Iraqi officers. At the time we were drawing down, and I had been put on a small team to inform the Iraqi army generals how to call their own helicopters for air support. Prior to this they would call the US Army, which would dispatch its Black Hawks.

Our goal was to teach them to be self-sufficient, and to accomplish this we would hold briefings and training on the current systems. One day we had set up the meeting for 0800 and waited patiently. Finally, around 1100, one Iraqi colonel showed up. He informed us the others Iraqi officers were not coming. Trying to not waste the opportunity we asked him to have a seat so we could at least train him. "The day is shot," he stated. I looked at my watch, "But it's 1100," I replied. "The day is shot," was his response, then he turned and walked out.

It took us multiple days to finally accomplish the training we had set out to do. I learned patience, to play on their timeline, and to not force things. I won't get into politics, but it came down to watching the Iraqis do it our way until the money dried up. They then disconnected from our procedures and handled it their way, and I don't blame them. The younger generation was more westernized, and I hope that someday that will take hold.

There were a lot of frustrating times while I was over there, but I learned a lot because I listened. Remember to always listen, which is one of the hardest things to do.

Don't be a social tragedy, you ARE resilient

Let me begin with this: no matter what anybody says, or what you think about yourself even at this very moment, you matter. Today there is study after study about social media and its effects on people. Suicide rates

are up and social bullying is being highlighted. I often think to myself, "Whatever happened to 'sticks and stones will break my bones but words will never hurt me'?"

Resilient—what exactly does that mean? Here's Webster's definition:

A person able to withstand or recover quickly from difficult conditions
or
(of a substance or object) able to recoil or spring back into shape after bending, stretching, or being compressed.

If you haven't paid attention to any of the pictures, I'm a ginger. My hair was a strawberry blond growing up, so naturally I would get teased about it. I didn't let it affect me. Sure, it wasn't fun, but at the end of the day, I had my family and friends. I have attended a multitude of military training schools. If you look at my resume, it seems like I was looking to get yelled at and belittled and stressed out. Let's take a look at it again:

Basic Training
Tech School
Officer Training School
Pilot Training
Aircraft Commander Upgrade
Instructor Upgrade

In addition to the formal schools I was subjected to countless check rides and other events in which high stress is involved. Basic training wasn't super fun. I was the guide so I had extra marching practice. At one point I was having so much trouble with a turn that the TI (Training Instructor) showed his class ring and told me he was going to punch it through my thigh.

One stressful situation came during basic training as we were having a locker inspection. I made sure my towels were folded correctly and my shirts were ironed with the correct spacing between hangers. I was all set.

The TI began at the end of the row as each of us stood at attention. He would go through each trainee's locker and note the demerits for each incorrect item, such as a shirt was folded wrong, there was lint on your blues pants, whatever it was. They didn't let anything slide, and their attention to detail was astounding.

Shortly after beginning my row, the TI started yelling at one of the trainees a couple of lockers down from me. In his best voice of the Count from *Sesame Street* I heard him begin, "*One* folded wrong—ha, ha, ha; *two* folded wrong—ha, ha, ha." This continued for about five items. I heard him move over to the next locker, where he again found items incorrectly placed.

Finally, it was my turn. The day didn't seem to be going well for anybody, so I wasn't expecting much better. During the inspection you were only allowed a certain number of demerits or your locker would fail. I don't remember what the number was, but let's say it was three.

The TI started going through my stuff, then finally arrived at my towels. He noted one of them to be incorrectly folded. This put me over the limit. I had failed my locker room inspection. Still to this day I don't know how I had the guts—or maybe it was stupidity—to do what I did next. Maybe in heaven God will let me watch the replay, but after the TI was a couple of lockers farther down, I got up the courage and stupidity to report in: "Airman Golembiewski reporting," I stated.

The TI immediately stopped mid inspection and slowly turned around with lasers in his eyes. You would have thought somebody had stolen his baby.

"What did you say?" he stated in a deathly tone.

"Airman Golembiewski reporting," I said again.

"What?" he snapped back.

"Sir," my voice a little shaky now, "my towel is folded correctly, sir."

"What!?" the TI yelled back, and made a beeline to my locker. He didn't even stop, he just began grabbing everything, chucking it all over the place while screaming, "One demerit, two demerits," and so on.

After he completely emptied it out, the barracks looked like a yard sale. Then came the best part. He came running back to me screaming, "Bubble locker! That is a bubble locker. You have one hour to clean it up and I'm

coming back. And if you get so much as one demerit, you are gone!"
If there was ever a time to pee my pants, that felt like it, but I held it
together. The TI stormed out, forgetting to inspect the last few lockers.
The guys helped me gather up my things and helped me prepare for my
re-inspection in less than an hour. I'm not sure what was going on behind
closed doors, but the re-inspection never came that day. But I'll tell you
what—I was shaking in my boots that whole day.

I like to think I'm pretty resilient, and I know you are too. Resiliency
is a state of mind. Very rarely does it involve anything physical. It is all
psychological, and guess what? You have 100 percent control over your
mind. Think about that! There is no mind-control device. Nobody can tap
into your head and take over.
 Your body, on the other hand, is different. Just because your mind says
you can dunk doesn't mean you can. Take care of your mind. If you are
having trouble with social media and being attacked, you can turn off the
app. Shields up, Scotty!

It reminds me of the movie *Ralph Breaks the Internet.* Ralph has just
posted all sorts of videos online to help make money to save the day.
He walks into the comments room and starts seeing all the negative
comments about him. It angers and depresses him.

In the words of Cypher in *The Matrix*, "Ignorance is bliss." And in this
case, it is. I also have a reality check for you too. You know all those
glamour shots? Great. Vacation pictures and cute pictures of puppies?
Those people have problems too. No one's life is perfect. Just look at all
the movie stars and rich people that get arrested, or drink themselves silly.
You think they have it perfect? They don't.

Being resilient will help you get through tough times, and if you find
yourself in a dark place, reach out for a friend's hand. Someone will catch
you. The beauty of the Air Force is if you are having a tough time with
something, there are a number of programs to help you out if you don't
want to go to friends or family. In my experience, it's always better to go
with your friends and family, but everyone's situation is different. Every
airman we lose means others have to take their place, and the world needs
airmen.

Yeah ... we're going to be simulating that today

During my time at F. E. Warren AFB, the unit had recently been qualified to fire weapons from the aircraft. The only authorized weapon was the M240 machine gun. In order to become qualified to fly with weapons on board, I had a training sortie. Not only to improve our skills at flying gun patterns but also to maintain what we called currency, we would fly training sorties out to the gun range.

This was one of my first training flights as I was being upgraded to be qualified in aerial gunnery as a pilot. The range was a spot of land owned and utilized by the Army. There they had placed many old armored vehicles, armored personnel carriers, and storage containers. These ancient relics were our targets.

During a typical flight you would fly to the range, set up some clearing passes, warm up the guns, and then proceed to enter multiple types of gun patterns, picking out targets and shooting at them. We would load the ammo in the cans, set them in the aircraft, then proceed out to the range and expend all the rounds. Each flight engineer had a quota they were required to fire every so many months to stay qualified. If this didn't occur, they would become overdue and were required to fly with an instructor to become current.

This particular day started off differently. We were told there was no ammo for us to use. We had run out, and it would be a few days before the next shipment arrived. The flight was still important for the pilots to accomplish, but we didn't need to fire actual rounds from the aircraft. We were authorized to "simulate" the weapons being fired.

We took off and headed out to a local area, choosing a random field since there was no need for the range. We set up a gun pattern around a local abandoned farmhouse. I briefed the pattern, informed which side was going to be firing, then headed in on the run. I called, "open fire" over the intercom. "Pew, pew, pew, pew," came from my gunner as he simulated firing on the house. (This made the *Lego Batman* movie even more entertaining for me.) All my initial training was handled this way, and multiple currency sorties exercised the same way. I had been excited at the thought of firing weapons from the aircraft, but that would have to wait.

In the USAF helicopter world, previously only our Pave Hawks had weapons, and it had taken over twenty years to get authorization to add that capability to the Huey. This was new, fascinating stuff to a lot of us, especially the old hats like myself who had only flown Hueys their whole career.

Shortly after this event, I was again scheduled for a live-fire sortie. All the standard briefings occurred, and we began our flight toward the range. The whole journey I was thinking, "What's it going to sound and feel like when they start firing?"

Thoughts of movies, loud gun sounds, and explosions were spinning in my mind. Then I remembered that movies sensationalized war scenes (Michael Bay EXPLOSIONS!), and I determined that because of our double hearing protection, ear plugs, and helmet, it really will sound like pew, pew, pew.

We arrived at the gun range, contacted the range controller, then cleared the range, looking for any wildlife, people, or anything else that would cause us to have to delay or cancel. Then, after much anticipation, I announced, "Clear to arm."

The flight engineers on each side responded with "Clear to arm," followed by "Right side ready to fire," then "Left side ready to fire." Straight and level, ready for the warm-up gun run I announced, "Open fire," and waited for *pew, pew, pew*. What I got was a *POW, POW, POW.* Those suckers were loud. It *was* like the movies! It was crazy loud, and not at all what I had determined in my mind it would be like. There was no simulation that could have prepared me for that.

As my career progressed, we went from training to actually doing everything to simulating nearly everything. Recurring training went from class sessions to CBTs (Computer-Based Training), and exercises went from doing the task to acting it out to just talking it out.

Throughout the later portion of my career, this was extremely frustrating. It's something you have to deal with, but I was always asking to simulate less as there is valuable experience gained by actually doing certain tasks. You can only simulate so far. Budget has been the driving

factor for many of the simulation issues, but also safety has had an increased role.

Finding the fine line between safety and getting good training can be very difficult. Try your best to not get frustrated and find creative ways to make it as close to real as possible in your training, then make those suggestions to your training managers. Pew, pew, pew!

Helmet, check . . . Checklist, check . . . Emotions packed away, check . . .

One of our new aircraft commanders was standing at the ops desk looking over some paperwork. When he saw me, he pointed out the schedule for the day, which was labeled with all the different flights for the day. Typically, there was a morning launch, afternoon launch, and evening launch. This day wasn't much different in any aspect except one.

"We're on a three-ship." The AC perked up.

"Who's flight lead?" I asked. He shrugged his shoulders, and I turned to review the schedule.

The flight lead designation would usually be given to the most senior crew in those days, but it was missed so none of the crews were identified as the lead. I looked at the AC.

"I've never flown a three-ship before," he stated, and I could tell by his voice he was a little excited.

"You're lead," I responded. A look of sheer terror fell over his face. Had this been a movie, I think he would have passed out. He reiterated that he had never flown a three-ship formation before, and I informed him that's why he was going to plan it. Remember, you learn from stress and failure, and this would be a good test to see how he could adapt.

After a few minutes, I found the AC I had tasked with being flight lead, and he agreed on a time for the flight briefing. I gathered up my crew and headed into the briefing room, where we met up with the other two aircraft crews. After our standard beginnings, the time hack and such, our

flight lead began the briefing. He went over the sequence of events, the landing zones we would be landing in, and all the while I would point out mistakes and make suggestions. The flight lead was becoming more defeated by the minute.

After the briefing, we all left to grab our flight gear, then headed to the aircraft. As I was strapping into the seat, I noticed our director of operations walking toward the aircraft. I waited to see where he was going as we were the farthest aircraft from the hangar door. I hung my helmet back on the hook as he passed the second aircraft. I was trying to think what he was coming to talk to me about; maybe one of the other aircraft broke? But then why wouldn't he have just called on the radio? He approached, and I leaned out the door of the Huey.

"You guys are going to go as a two-ship; I don't think your flight lead is mentally stable enough to execute the flight."

I was taken aback; it never occurred to me that this would ever happen. Having our plan in place minus one ship, we started up and flew the sortie.

Upon landing I sought out the AC to further discuss the preparation for the flight. The big problem was he had been overwhelmed by the added planning he had to do for the extra aircraft, and his first mistake was not asking for help. He attempted to do it alone.

Remember, life is a team sport; the Air Force is a team sport. No matter what job you have, where you are, or what you are doing, you have help. I did not restrict his use of the rest of the crew, and as I mentioned, I had very little to do prior to the briefing. Had he asked for assistance or advice, I would have gladly given it to him. There are a bunch of takeaways, and here's the big thing I learned that day: the environment is always adapting, and as a leader/instructor/supervisor/teacher, you have to adapt with it.

I treated the AC as I had been treated when I was a junior aviator, and my overcoming that stress and utilizing all my surroundings was how I managed to learn and grow. As with many events in life, the right amount of stress will make you grow.

Take bodybuilding, for example. If you only lifted light weights, and with very few reps, your muscles wouldn't grow. It's only the added stress that tears the muscle fibers so the body adapts, heals, and comes back stronger. As you are put through stressful situations you will grow, but also know there will be an end. It can't go on forever.

Through this experience I learned to pay better attention to an individual's personality, notice when I was bringing them to the tipping point, and then back off. When you are put into a situation like that, control your emotions.

We have all been there, and seeing the big picture can help you realize how small any one issue is. Had the AC let it go and we flew as planned, there would have been no issues. I wasn't going to ground him, fail him, and take away his wings. And I guarantee his crew would have helped him through it. He lost valuable training that day by not keeping his emotions in check and becoming resilient.

You're landing where?

It was a beautiful fall day—not a cloud in the sky. I was flying over the missile fields, skipping from one missile launch facility to another. The wind was blowing pretty good but nothing more than I had seen before. We would often use it to see how fast of a ground speed we could get—sometimes upwards of 160 knots (184 mph).

My crew was one of the newest, and my copilot was a very interesting guy to fly with. He was an avid hunter and would repeatedly see a speck in the distance and call out, "That's a mallard duck." There was no way I could tell that without binoculars, but I would let it go.

My flight engineer was our newest. He ended up becoming a pilot later in his career, and the last I had heard he was flying V-22 Ospreys. Nearing the end of the sortie, we received a call for the base. It was reported to be an outer zone alarm going off at one of the launch facilities that held a Minuteman nuclear missile.

This being one of my first flights as an aircraft commander, I was excited at the prospect of finding something out of the ordinary at the site. Typically,

it would be a deer, rabbit, or sometimes melting snow that triggered the alarm. I accomplished all of the required planning, calculated fuel, loiter time, the whole shebang. We could make it but would only have enough fuel to make one pass then return to base.

We proceeded to the site and found . . . nothing. A big nothing. So, we turned and headed home. Everything was going well, but about halfway back I noticed the fuel gauge was lower than anticipated. I ran some more calculations, and sure enough, we were not going to make it to base.

How could this be? I had calculated everything. What was going on? Had we had a fuel issue? Nope, we had a 40 mph headwind, and I hadn't calculated for that. I tried to figure out a course of action and came up with landing at the downtown airport. It was in a direct line in between the base and our current location, and per my calculations, we could just make it.

As we continued on our way, I tried every trick I could think of, short of shutting one of the engines down. The fuel continued to dwindle lower and lower. Soon we were under 200 pounds which, was our mandatory fuel quantity to land with. We were still a ways off, and the hairs were starting to really stand up on the back of my neck. Eighty pounds . . . almost there!

Once over the airport, I continued to keep up our speed all the way to parking and landed with sixty pounds indicated, well below our mandatory two hundred. I messed up, and I messed up bad, but by the grace of God I was able to make it to the airport.

I remember the operations supervisor trying to convince me to just fly the final five miles to base. Not wanting to transmit my actual fuel state, I elected to take the conservative action and live to fight another day. I called the operations supervisor, and we refueled and headed back home for my hot date—in my commander's office!

I knew it was coming and tried to take it in stride. I explained the whole situation, my decision-making, and how I would never do that again. My commander verbally reprimanded me but also commended me on safely landing as opposed to tempting fate and trying to cover up the issue. This

was a far cry from that day at tech school when I turned myself in. I was going to punish myself enough, and being in the aircrew world, I knew I would never live it down, but I was OK with that.

Learn from your mistakes. You will make plenty throughout your career. The important thing is that you learn from them, correct them, and move on. Also, don't think that getting more experience will make you mistake-proof.

One experience I learned a lot from came during the dead of winter in Washington State. The tallest peak in our training area to the north was Calispell Peak. At the summit was a radio station, and the previous day there had been a large snowfall that covered up the radio antennas. These antennas were used as a radio relay station not only for us but also for the survival instructors.

Due to the heavy snowfall, the radio transmissions were having issues, and the ice and snow could further damage the equipment. This would occasionally happen throughout the winter, and the quickest way to take care of the situation was for us to fly a couple troops and their trusty brooms up to the station. I had been there plenty of times before, but it was my first winter in the mountains, a drastic change from the fields of North Dakota.

We gathered up our gear and calculated numbers for the amount of fuel we could carry to safely land at the LZ. The day was gorgeous, the sun was shining, the storm had completely passed through, and it looked like it was going to be a great day to fly.

We finished prepping our aircraft, and in short order we were climbing out of the Tacoma command post on our mission. It was a short flight to the peak, maybe fifteen minutes or so, and I was flying with one of our new copilots. I had him fly the first portion of the sortie and determined it would be very beneficial for him to gain more experience by flying the whole approach in to the LZ.

Our procedures at the time were to fly over the landing location at 300 feet and check a myriad of things, such as size, shape of the LZ, and wind direction. My copilot verbally accounted for all the items, and I had no

problem with his assessment, so we continued on. He determined a steep approach would afford him the best go-around options, and I agreed.

We began the approach like normal, slowed down the airspeed, and began our descent to the LZ. As we moved closer to the peak, I noticed we were getting lower than we needed to be. I made some verbal corrections, my copilot acknowledged, and I assumed he had started to correct. We continued to get lower until our eyes were level with the top of the mountain. I realized that I had let us go too far, and we were facing immediate impact with the ground as we continued to sink.

I checked our power; the copilot had already given it all we had sitting at 100 percent. Realizing we were in a tight spot, I quickly grabbed the controls, announced that I had the aircraft, and swiftly turned away from the mountain.

The trees rushed up at us as my flight engineer was calling tree heights: "Five feet, four feet, three feet, two feet." I quickly glanced out my side window; the tree tops were eye-level. What was he talking about? There was no way it was even close to two feet. It was way less.

We continued down the mountain side, my rotor blades spinning very near the trees, power at 102 percent. I couldn't add any more or things would go from bad to worse. I made slight turns, navigating in between the lowest trees, until finally the terrain dropped off more steeply, and I was in the clear.

The crisis was averted, and after we all relaxed a bit, I asked my flight engineer what he was talking about on his height calls. The standard practice was to call the ground or obstacle for the distance of our skid tubes and our landing gear, but he had been calling it from the main rotor blades up top.

After some discussion, we climbed above the mountaintop to assess what had gone wrong. We threw some smoke out, thinking the wind had played a role. It was calm with no wind, which was surprising.

After some analysis, we determined that more than likely we just didn't have enough power to hover without the ground near us, which resulted

in a term we called "settling with power." We reattempted but this time chose a different path to the site and landed with no problems. I had made the mistake of not correcting my copilot soon enough, and it almost cost us.

I learned plenty that day and would later attend a mountain flying course in Canada to learn all the mistakes we had made during that flight. You will find yourself on that "mistake" side of the equation plenty of times, but it's also important to understand the other side. As an instructor, I loved it when my students would fail. I would try to make them fail, or put them in situations they had to figure out. I know this may come across as being sort of a jerk, but we all learn much quicker from failure.

Another time I was holding alert at the survival school and launched on a mission to help find a lost student. During survival training there is a phase where the students will be given coordinates to navigate to, but to simulate a threat environment, they must do it without being seen. The survival instructors would act as hostiles and search for the students. After a specified amount of time, the students would all check in at the rally point, and the scenario would be over.

On this day there were two missing students. We were called out to help search for them from the air. We launched like normal, and I was with a young copilot. I managed the flight the way I always did, having him fly the majority of the search patterns. Our flight engineer was searching from one door, and sometimes we would have a medic on board doing the same out the other side.

After some time, our engineer announced that he thought he spotted something. I marked the map and GPS and instructed the copilot to come around and put the aircraft into a hover so we could get a better look. He made his turn and proceeded inbound on the approach. As our forward progress slowed to a stop, I noticed the nose of the aircraft move sightly right, then it continued moving more. I checked our hover power; no issues arose, and I waited to see where this was going to go.

The nose continued to swing to the right, and by now it was gaining speed. We were now ninety degrees off from the initial heading where we began. I waited a split second longer, and the spin continued. We were like a

merry-go-round, in mid-air. I asked in a very inquisitive voice, "What are you going to do?" It was at this point I saw my copilot correct his feet on the pedals and pushed in the left pedal to control the spin. He was able to get it mostly under control as I helped him with the inputs to correct the spinning motion.

The rest of that trip his pedal control was impeccable. He had learned from his failure and knew the consequences. As much fun as it was spinning like a top, it was not a good thing and could have led to something pretty horrible. As you become a supervisor, or in my case also an instructor, remember to let your people fail—within reason, of course.

No excuses! Play like a champion!

When I was growing up playing sports, my dad always pushed me to work harder and be better. If I failed or struggled, I would get up and do it again. That's how you learn to ride a bike. You get going, fall, realize falling sucks, and try harder the next time. In life and the Air Force it's the same.

One of the sports I fell in love with later in life was ice hockey. While I grew up on a lake, skating every winter, I never had a strong desire to play it competitively, at least in the sense of an organized league. I finally decided to jump into it in high school and immediately wished I had done it sooner.

I still play to this day in a local recreational league and with friends throughout the country in adult tournaments. During games, the beginning is always great—you are fresh, lots of energy, spirits are high, everything is going great. The honeymoon phase, as they say. But soon you begin to throttle back, and putting all that effort into skating seems to be going nowhere. You lose focus and drive, then that's when bad things happen. Playing in my rec hockey league is no different. As the game progresses, fatigue begins to set in.

Due to my competitive nature, I have two speeds: stop and full tilt. I've been working on the middle portion and have been getting better at it. What I'm guilty of is not checking myself and starting off too fast like I've been shot out of a cannon.

This is always great at first, but then as the game goes along, I begin to get fatigued, and I start to cut corners and get lazy. If I expend too much energy too early, I begin to not pick my skates up off the ice as much. This has led to more than once catching an edge and hurting my pride as I plummeted to the ice. In addition, I find myself not hustling after a loose puck and missing out on it, by sometimes inches. So, what am I getting at?

Professional athletes work at their craft every day, and it becomes so automatic for them that it looks effortless. They know how much energy to exert, the right times to throttle back, and the times to put the pedal to the metal. In your career, whatever it may be, you need to become a master of this. There will be times where you are on autopilot, and putting in too much effort is like banging your head against the wall.

Then there will be times when extra effort is needed. For example, sending that extra clarification email, while time-consuming, could help avoid possible larger issues down the road. Or maybe you need to buckle down and finish an awards package in one sitting, allowing more time for it to be processed.

When we fail or have issues, it's human nature to say, "Woe is me," and put the blame somewhere else. Some people do this with everything. Not only does this mentality hurt you, but it also hurts your peers, family, and friends. This attitude is infectious in a bad way and can lead to less effort and poor performance in all we do. Throw away the excuses and play like a champion. There are always roadblocks. There are always things that you must overcome, but don't let that dissuade you from moving forward.

I seem to find the hard way to do nearly everything. One example was my desire to fly fixed wing again for fun. I had convinced my wife to allow us to find and purchase a small plane. I wanted it to be a twin engine for the added safety since I would be flying with my family. In the civilian world in order to fly a multi-engine aircraft, you have to have a multi-engine rating ,which I did. I had taken a written exam after pilot training and received my additional ratings, such as helicopter, instrument, and multi-engine.

However, there was a catch to the multi-engine. I had flown the T-37 in Phase One of UPT which was a multi-engine jet trainer. The catch was

that due to the engines being close to the fuselage (like so many fighter aircraft), my certificate for multi-engine was restricted to centerline thrust.

This meant to fly a civilian multiengine, unless it was a fighter-like aircraft, I would have to take a check ride, performing multi-engine emergency maneuvers such as shutting down an engine and landing single engine. While I could have paid an FAA evaluator, rented a plane, and flown a check ride, I didn't feel comfortable doing so without some practice. So I found a multi-engine aircraft and instructor about an hour's drive away.

Over the course of a few months, I flew a total of eight hours, spending some good coin to get ready for my check ride. I scheduled the check ride, things went well, and I passed. After that, the evaluator submitted the paperwork, and my restriction was removed. I was authorized to fully fly multi-engine airplanes. Now fast-forward to less than a year after I accomplished all of that, the FAA decided to simply remove that restriction. It no longer exists.

So, while I would have done some lessons to refresh my hands, I wouldn't have had the added stress of a check ride. But I persevered, and in the end I'm better for it. I learned a lot, and while it was a tough road, it was worth it.

I could have made excuses to not accomplish my goal, sitting at home and doing nothing, but I pushed through that fear and doubt. Doubt is what stops us from playing like a champion. Fear sets in. We make excuses about why we can't do it, see only the roadblocks, and give up. You can do anything you set your sights on. You can make a difference, and you can motivate others around you.

Have you ever known a person or friend who when they come in the room, is full of energy and joy? When things don't go their way, they take it in stride. Some of you are probably thinking, "Yeah, and I'd like to punch them in the face."

Ever notice, though, how infectious it is, how it motivates you to maybe chase your dreams or excel, only to find that when they leave, you lose that drive? I guarantee they don't have it all together, and it frustrates them just like it would

you when things don't go their way, but they push through it and get things done. I've been told a few times that I never seem overstressed when things don't go according to plan. Does it bother and frustrate me? No doubt! But stewing in my own rage has never helped the situation and, more often than not, has made it worse. I didn't always take things in stride; it is definitely a learned skill. I effectively lost a friend because of it once.

During my tour at Fairchild, I was one of the senior instructor pilots and had also been acting as the assistant director of operations (ADO). We had a lot of training to keep track of, and the unit had become a little loose with briefing times. This meant that less-than-stellar plans were being briefed for each sortie. My background as a schoolhouse instructor kicked in, and I was motivated to fix the issue.

I sat down and created very detailed briefings, sent them to all the pilots, and then briefed them myself. Leading by example was what I was going for. Well, on this fateful day, I had asked one of the other instructors to be flight lead and brief the sortie. He gathered up all the information, built the plan, then briefed it.

I was beside myself. The briefing was done very poorly, the details were missing, and this happened to be the third or fourth briefing in a row I had attended that wasn't done very professionally. I ripped into him, in front of both crews, and boy, was that a mistake. I had let all the frustration build up and let it all loose, not only at a friend and a fellow instructor, but in front of half the flight.

Afterwards I was pulled aside, and my friend told me how small I had made him feel in front of everyone, and I instantly regretted the actions I had taken. I should have discussed the issues about the briefing one-on-one, but instead I made a spectacle of it. Our relationship was never the same, and I regret the way I handled the situation to this day.

The next time you're feeling frustrated with your roadblock, take a step back and look at the situation from all angles. And remember it's like the quote from the movie *The Hangover Part II* "But did you die?" It could always be worse unless you're dead, and then I'm not sure how you're reading this, but OK.

G's lessons learned

This is probably my favorite topic of the book. I learned a lot from my physical journey, going through my fat phase and eventually getting into shape. Failing at multiple different tasks and being able to overcome it. As I stated already, grit and determination win out 99 percent of the time, and I say ninety-nine because nothing really is ever 100 percent.

Never give up; keep pushing forward. Get started, (that's the hardest part), and once you do, you will see how easy the next step is. I equate it to Newton's law of momentum, which is true not only in physics but in emotions, motivation, and determination: an object at rest stays at rest, and an object in motion stays in motion. And in some instances, it picks up speed.

Start your motion now. Don't wait until the perfect time—it may never come.

Do it now.

CHAPTER FOUR: ADAPTED

__Adapt__- become adjusted to new conditions.
["a large organization can be slow to __adapt to__ change"]

This chapter covers your adaptability and how prepared you are for the challenges ahead. As an airman you are thrown into tasks and missions that require preparation and planning. The more you have, the better, but you must also be flexible enough to adapt. As our Air Force studies teach us, flexibility is the key to air power. Semper Gumby.

Questions to ask yourself:

- Question 1: How do you prepare for a task? Are you a procrastinator, or do you plan ahead?
- Question 2: How can you better prepare yourself, and what are the different outcomes when you do?
- Question 3: How well do you adapt to change, and what can you do to enhance that?

The pace of progress and proper planning

In the words of Helmuth Von Moltke, "No good plan survives first contact with the enemy."

You will hear this a lot throughout your career. No matter how well you plan or your unit thinks they plan, it never goes on time or the way it was scheduled. I have seen this in all sorts of events, from building plans to training events. The big mantra is there's not enough time, but a lot of that stems from procrastination and not looking forward to the end game.

If you want to set yourself up for success, plan ahead of everyone else. Be prepared for the dreaded last-minute tasks that always seem to come out of nowhere. I was continually frustrated with this and have heard plenty of others having the same issues.

It seems we are constantly putting out fires because we never seem to plan far enough in advance. If people do plan in advance, it isn't an issue until the deadline is closing in to a breaking point. Work to plan ahead,

and be the squeaky wheel asking how projects are coming along. Let your supervisor know when an event is going to occur so they are not caught off guard.

For all the meetings commanders and staff have detailing the agenda, it's surprising how many things come down to the wire, but they do. Expect them before a three-day weekend, or when you're going on leave, or at the end of the day. If you have a good supervisor, they will understand you stayed late working on a project, and can let you report late the following day or another predetermined day. When you become a supervisor, don't forget that, especially if the tasking is coming directly from you. Expect to be frustrated, but know that it will be over soon and things will get back to normal.

What Hollywood got right

Six months into my deployment to Iraq I found myself in a very interesting situation. As previously described, I was the Iraqi Helicopter Operations Advisor. On a daily basis, I would ride with a few other advisors to the Iraqi Air Force headquarters, which happened to be Saddam's zoo when he was in power.

It was a very interesting place. They had converted all the buildings to offices, and most of the water features were nearly dried up. I would meet every day with my counterpart to discuss how things were going, what were the plans for training pilots, and how they would be added to the operational units.

Then one day I received word that the helicopter section had moved. I was a little confused; had they moved offices? Nope, they had moved completely to the other side of Baghdad in the Green Zone.

The joy of the whole situation was I moved into the Green Zone as well. (A smidge of sarcasm there.) This whole move stemmed from Iraqi history. During Saddam's reign, the helicopters were their separate command, and we had tried to lump them with the Iraqi fixed-wing guys. They apparently didn't like it and wanted to go back to the old structure. So, after the move, I found myself with two other advisors to support a whole branch of the military. No pressure, right?

My days were spent driving in an armored Rhino over to the Iraqi Helicopter Command headquarters every day and moving between seven shops ranging from logistics to training to operations. One day we were informed that they had found equipment to add rockets to their Mi-17s. Not only had they started modifying their Mi-17s, but in less than a week they were going to have a test firing.

Being in the USAF for some time, I knew how we would accomplish this. There would be dry firing, testing, ground fires, more testing, aerial practice, more testing, and then a live-fire test in the air. Generally something like that, and I assumed they would do the same. After all, they had been learning from us for the past seven years.

A day or two later I was shown some photos of the rocket modifications they had added to their aircraft. Having worked electronics, I was assuming it would be relatively clean wiring, some cannon plugs and connectors. Nope, the pictures I was shown had bare multistrand copper wire hand twisted together with no shielding. Oh, and after I was shown this wiring (which they were very proud of, by the way), I was told they were accomplishing an aerial testing in a few days.

At this point I didn't think anything would surprise me; boy, was I wrong. When I asked how they were going to test it, they informed me it would be during a live-fire, multiservice exercise utilizing live ground troops and artillery. What?! They hadn't even test-fired anything, and they were going to test their rockets with troops on the ground!

After a failed attempt to convince them to do a test fire beforehand, I sat back and hoped it would all go well. I was asked to accompany them to the exercise, which would be held in the desert away from any major city, and they would have a viewing area for us all to watch the event.

I worked the system and was given approval to fly in the Iraqi Hueys out to the exercise location. On the day of the event, we headed to the helipad and awaited the Hueys. They arrived as scheduled. We boarded, and were off flying over Baghdad, then farmer' fields, and eventually the desert.

On the way, the aircraft would randomly fire off defensive flares that were installed and set on auto dispense. This was a little disconcerting, but I

later found out that the reflection of the sun in some of the ponds we were flying over was enough for the system to think it was a missile being shot at the aircraft and deploy the flares.

We eventually made it to the location of the exercise and deboarded the helicopter. Then I found myself on what felt like a Hollywood set. In my head I assumed they would have some chairs set up, but no, it was like you see in the movies, tents all decked out. Inside were refreshment tables, couches, coffee tables—the whole works. It was crazy. We arrived a little early, so we mingled with the command staff, then took our seats for the big show.

The band started playing (yes, they had a band) and then the announcer started. My translator described everything. First, the artillery would begin the attack. At that point you could hear the artillery pieces firing, and in short order you could see the explosions. It was like having front row tickets to a sporting event. We were at the centerline, the opposing team was to the right, and our attacking force was to the left heading right.

After the artillery stopped firing, the announcer chimed in again. The ground forces would begin their assault along with the aerial rocket attack by the Mi-17s. I watched as troops emerged from the left, heading to the right. Then they showed up—two Mi-17s on the horizon—and I prayed that everything would go well. No sooner had the Mi-17s arrived directly over the ground forces they opened fire. Rockets went everywhere, luckily most of them straight, and the others that strayed off target didn't go too far off the play area. This was a surreal experience.

What I learned from the experience is to never assume anything. And while the Iraqis had little expertise in technology, they were very creative and could make things work. There will be times that you are surprised, but prepare yourself as best you can.

The Iraqis thought outside the box to get their aircraft configured to fire weapons. I never saw the final product up close, but they were able to engineer it to work properly, at least for that day.

Use your creative thinking to enhance your job. I'm not saying we had to twist wires together, but if you come up with a new solution to a problem,

be sure to pass it along to your supervisor. Your solution may move the project forward quicker than anyone anticipated, and that's a plus because in the Air Force things tend to move slowly.

I'm traveling the world

I slowly followed the crowd down the aisle of the 747 to the exit door. Upon reaching it, I was hit with the brightest light known to man. I put on my sunglasses and continued squinting as I walked down the ramp. We had just landed in Qatar, the holding tank for all personnel going in and out of Iraq. The concrete was incredibly bright, and it felt like the sun was right on top of me. I went through the processing line, then headed to my air-conditioned tent. It was ninety degrees in there, but I guess at least it was shaded and not 105 degrees.

I was on my way to my tour in Baghdad; it was my turn to go. A few months earlier I had been approached by my commander, who informed me I was in the hot seat for deployment, number one on the list in my career field, actually. So I had two choices. I could decline the deployment or request a certain assignment and have a good chance of getting it by volunteering. This is one of those times I was "voluntold" to accept an assignment.

My commander gave me a couple days to decide, and I had a discussion

with my wife. We were in a unique situation as she was also active duty and in the same career field, and our commander at Minot was able to work out a joint assignment for us. The Air Force is very good about working with couples, and we had the luxury of always being stationed together.

To give you a broader picture of the landscape, this was 2010; the US Government had been in Iraq for years and was attempting to rebuild the Iraqi military. Deployments were rampant at the time. We were sending advisor after advisor over there for one-year tours. Some of the simpler jobs were three to six months, but all the positions I could fill were year-long deployments.

After some discussion with my wife, I convinced her to volunteer with me. This would reset both our deployment clocks, and then we wouldn't have the threat of deployment for some time. This would allow us to have a family when we returned and have a little stability figuring out kids.

I went to my commander and gave him our dream deployment options in order. First, we would like to be deployed at the same time, which we ended up getting. Well, almost. My wife ended up leaving a little over a month before me, but not bad so far. Second was the ability to serve at the same location, which we got for a month. (More details on that later.) Third, we requested a flying assignment, which ended up being a big nada for both of us.

On my arrival in Baghdad, I found myself in the hottest and brightest place I had ever been. I felt like I was melting and was thankful I had gotten into good shape before deploying. This was only my second time being overseas, the first being my honeymoon in Germany, and no, I'm not counting Canada. Even my recruiter told me not to put that on my MEP forms because everyone from Michigan has been to Canada. Fun fact: Did you know Michigan is the only state north of Canada? Look it up—totally true.

Back to my arrival in Qatar. The customs agents were grumpy, I dragged my four bags of gear everywhere (three of which I never used), and I slept in a ninety-degree tent. A few days later I hopped on a C-130 and landed in Baghdad.

In today's world, all our deployments take us to hot desert climates. Gone are the jungle wars, at least for now, so I would do some research on the Middle Eastern culture. It is vastly different from Western culture, as I learned from that deployment. Overall, I think if we could install air-conditioning over there, everyone would be happy.

During the summer months, mortar attacks were a daily occurrence, then during winter not a peep, but as soon as the hot weather hit, it was "Fire the missiles!" I just think they hated the heat. All joking aside, I believe we are going to be in the Middle East for the long term, and if you deploy, that's more than likely where you'll be, so study up.

As for traveling to multiple countries and seeing the world, that is a thing of the past with only a few exceptions. If you joined or you want to join the Air Force to travel the world, you need to know what you're getting yourself into.

In basic training the big joke was that a quarter of the security forces members would never leave Texas because they were from there, they went to basic there, and they would be stationed there.

The same rings true in a lot of career fields. There are only certain locations where you can go, and sometimes it's hard to cross-train. A lot of careers are in the United States and don't really have many deployment options.

One example is missiles. In this career field you will be stationed stateside the whole time, and there will be very little opportunity for you to go overseas. On the other hand, if you're a mechanic—say on F-16s that are constantly deploying—you have a good chance to go overseas, but it will probably be to South Korea , so pay attention to where each career field is located.

Research will save you heartache down the line if you want to travel. If you have found yourself in a career field that doesn't travel much, you will have the option at the end of your first commitment to retrain. This is your best time to act. The longer you stay in one career, the harder it is to cross-train.

Off we go into the wild blue yonder

This section is for my pilots out there, whether you are one, want to be one, or are lined up for UPT. I was in Columbus, Mississippi, attending UPT. For those of us in my training class, it was nearing our drop night, which was only a couple of weeks away. During the drop night our fates would be decided by several different factors, including academic scores, flight grades, personality, commander input, and needs of the Air Force. Oh, and a touch of what we wanted as a student. All this would decide our career paths.

At the time, there were four tracks: the fighter track, the heavy track, the C-130 track, and the helicopter track. Our commander was all about fighters, which was quite humorous seeing he was a C-141 pilot. He always preached to go after the fighter track. I'm guessing that was the dream that he fell short of, and he wanted to live it through us.

At this time, I was still pursuing the same goal I had secretly shared with one of my classmates in the first days we were together. I was gunning for the helicopter slot. Things change over time, but at this point the competition was typically for the fighter slots, and the helicopter was the red-headed stepchild that nobody wanted.

This was no different in my class. I could almost feel the excitement of many of my classmates for having one less competitor for a fighter, not to mention they knew they wouldn't get stuck with the helicopter. My class agreed to keep it a secret from the instructors. I had heard that if the instructors found out you preferred helicopters, they would try and talk you out of it, and I was pretty dead set on flying "helos."

The previous day we had to submit our list ranked in order of what we wanted. Helicopters were at the top of my list, so I was anticipating some opposition to my decision. We had our morning routine, then we broke off to do a few different things.

I had finished my last check ride and a short extra credit, low-level orientation flight that everyone was scheduled to do. We were required to have a minimum number of hours to graduate UPT, and I

was a bit short. I'm sure it had to do with being "shot down" during a solo pattern sortie. Or at least that's what we would call it.

If during your solo flight around the airport you made a mistake, the instructor in the control tower would utter the phrase, "Make the next one a full stop." That was the verbal "surface to air missile," which meant you were immediately landing (shot down) and would have a briefing as to what you did wrong. I had been shot down on one previous ride, relatively quick, into the flight. The last hour I had to make up probably had a lot to do with that.

While a few of us were briefing for our extra sortie, one of the reserve pilots came in. He made a beeline right to me and sat down next to me. The gist of the conversation was him telling me, "Don't put helicopters on your list. You can't fly for the commercial airlines when you get out if you fly helicopters."

Thinking about this today makes me laugh. Due to the pilot shortage, airlines are paying helicopter pilots to get a fixed-wing certificate, then expediting their training to put them on the fast track to start making some serious cash. Funny how things change. I stuck to my guns and eventually reached my goal of flying helicopters and have never regretted it. Even with the events of the pandemic, the young crop of pilots is still lacking, and as air travel swings back once again, the need will be there. So I impress on you to follow your dream.

If you do get a heavy aircraft and want to fly fighters, there are ways, albeit slim, to also cross-train into that. As for the most important things to ensure you do during your flying career, here are a couple tips.

First, that civilian logbook you have, keep it in use and catalog all your flights if you have to. Write notes in it. I know it's a drag after a flight to fill out the Air Force forms and then sit down to write in another logbook. Guess what? You don't have to write. You can type or tap as well. Build an Excel sheet. I have an example on my website. Download it and adjust things for your categories or choose an app.

These are great because you can upload your certificated documents, take pictures of the AF 781, and have it wherever you go. Now, I know you're

asking, "Why would I do twice the work?" You would because the FAA and the military track things differently, and if you only let your military records speak for you, you're going to be missing out on a lot of flight time. Here are some examples:

- Air Force: Aircraft commander and copilot time are both logged based on your designation on your flight order.
- FAA: Pilot-in-command time (PIC) is logged anytime you are acting as the aircraft commander or touching the set of controls. Second-in-command time (SIC) is logged the rest of the flight.

How can this affect you? Let's say you're a copilot and you physically fly for one hour of a two-hour flight. If you looked at your military records, only your total flight time would be tracked as copilot time.

For example:
- AC=0 CO=2
- When you translate that over to the FAA, it becomes: PIC=0 SIC=2
- But you should log: PIC=1 SIC=1

So, by not tracking your own hours, you would miss out on one hour of flight time as PIC, and for all jobs in the civilian world, PIC time is the time that matters.

By putting in a little work today you will save yourself the headache tomorrow. I wish I had known that when I started flying. I didn't find that out until a few years before I retired. I was planning on getting a commercial pilot job and started compiling all my flight records, going through them line by line to determine what kind of sortie it was, and guessing as to the PIC time.

For a normal flight we would typically share a sortie, so as a copilot I would get half of the time as PIC time, but I know there were times I flew much longer. In addition to the PIC/SIC differences, mountainous time is big in the helicopter workforce, along with NVG time. Rules for Instrument Meteorological Conditions (IMC) and night also change every once in a while, so check out the FAA regulations to confirm you're logging it correctly.

Another recent change was that all taxi time counts as flight time in the civilian world. In the end, if you decide not to fly, not a big deal, but if you have even the slightest inkling of continuing your flying career when you separate, this will save you heartache and maybe even make you worth more to a potential employer.

What is your major malfunction?

Throughout your career you will be tasked with many things, some simple, some on a large, complex scale. As a leader I don't want to hear how hard it is or that you don't know how to do it. Just get it done. Maybe you don't know how to accomplish it, so find a solution. Ask a peer, find a mentor or a specialist, or try my favorite: YouTube University.

In flight operations we have an operations desk. This position is manned by one person who is in charge of tracking the aircraft flying, answering the phone, and running a myriad of checklists to ensure operations are running smoothly. You would think that in today's world with all the technology there would be an app or digital checklist to follow to make things easier. Well, our unit was still using a three-ring binder with checklists and wet-erase markers. Psst . . . paperless Air Force.

I approached the person in charge of the operations desk program and asked if they could digitize it, maybe on Excel, for example. The response I received was one I had often received during my last few years before retirement: "I don't have time and don't know how to do it." Does that sound like something you think your boss wants to hear?

I tried to look at it from his perspective. He had some other tasks, but nothing so time-consuming he couldn't devote a little time to the problem. The solution would actually reduce the amount of work his duty desk officers were doing, freeing up more time for other tasks.

On to his second rebuttal that he didn't know how to do it. Well, there are other individuals who know how to do it and then there is YouTube University. Ok so it's really just YouTube, but I have learned more on YouTube than I ever did in college. People post how to do everything on there.

Frustrated and to prove a point, I sat down with my computer and tried out a solution using some basic Excel skills, Google, and YouTube University. On a side note, be careful when proving points; it can end up with disastrous consequences. Remember to always think before you act. However, my situation didn't have any downsides as I saw it.

So I set myself to work and in one day I had rewritten the checklist, making it digital, adding notes and expounding on what each task involved. I even created links that would automatically send emails.

Was I super knowledgeable? Did I know how to do everything? Nope, I just used all the means at my disposal to execute and accomplish my task. Yes, it took some time to find the right video or article describing step-by-step instructions. Sometimes they didn't work at all, so I failed and moved on to another article that worked.

This is what your boss wants: a creative, autonomous, solution-bringing airman. I have had some amazing airmen at my disposal who would figure out a task I gave them without complaints or excuses, and they were selected for the next good deal. This will set you apart from your peers. You may even enjoy it.

There's something to be said about the pride you can feel when you see people utilizing a system you helped create, especially when it makes everyone's job easier. Now, I won't kid myself. There were flaws in the checklist I created, but over the next few months I saw it mature, get refined, and turned into a complete working product that reduced the time and frustration of the operations desk users.

G's lessons learned

You will hear it frequently: *Semper Gumby*. A joking reference to the animated character Gumby and the saying taught throughout Air Force training curriculums that flexibility is the key to airpower and is important not only on the battlefield. You'll hear plenty of other terms like this that simply mean one thing: adapt and overcome.

I was challenged with multiple different issues through my career, and no, I wasn't trained for them; and no, I don't have all the answers; and no, I'm not the smartest person in the room. I was resourceful, I found a way to get it done, I learned from my failures, and I changed the next outcome. You will need to adapt, go with the flow, change your way of thinking to a small extent.

Be prepared to hear the term *knee-jerk reaction*, but remember a quick reaction isn't always the right reaction. Do your research and due diligence. There are times when you have to react to your surroundings, and as humans, it is in our nature to take things as they come. But if you look ahead and plan, then when the time comes to implement something or adjust a procedure, you will be in a much better position to do so.

Be the ant, not the grasshopper.

CHAPTER FIVE: FAMILY/FRIENDS

Family - *a group of people related to one another by blood or marriage.*

This chapter covers the importance of family and friends. Whether married or single, your family and friends are a support structure that will motivate and help guide you through not only your career but your life. Take care of them, and they will take care of you.

Questions to ask yourself:

- Question 1: How well do you communicate with your family?
- Question 2: Are you signed up for programs and support to enable a good life for your family?
- Question 3: What can you do to better support those who love you?

I just got paid

In the movie *Jack Reacher*, Tom Cruise's character mentions four reasons people join the military:

"There are four types of people who join the military. For some, it's family trade. Others are patriots, eager to serve. Next you have those who just need a job. Then there's the kind who want the legal means of killing other people."

I fell into the "needing a job" category, something stable with a chance to provide for my potential family, as I was planning on marrying my girlfriend at the time within the next year.

The Air Force provided me with that option. While there would be risk involved—such as the potential for being away from family, not to mention being put in harm's way—one thing that would always be there was the paycheck. Even in the years of sequestration, the government always paid the military. Sorry, Coast Guard, I guess you don't count.

As a member of the Air Force not only will you get paid, but there are also bonuses for many jobs and some little-known programs, such as extra pay for individuals who speak another language fluently. If you speak Russian,

you can get paid just for that skill. You could go your whole career without utilizing that expertise, but your bank account will utilize it.

In addition, there are extra cost-of-living (COLA) allowances for living overseas, hazardous-duty pay, flight pay, and the list goes on. Research the many programs the Air Force has. I have mentioned some, but they are constantly changing and some new ones may pop up.

This isn't a financial book, but there are plenty of good ones out there, many of which I wish I had read when I was younger. As it was, I did participate in the Thrift Savings Plan (TSP), and if you do nothing else, at least utilize the TSP.

As a young lieutenant, I signed up, put 7 percent of my basic pay into it, and never thought about it again, except during tax time when my wife added the end-of-year statement to TurboTax. It was money that was hidden from me, and in the end, after about sixteen years of doing it, I ended up with $95,000 for retirement. If you do want good general savings practice, I would refer you to the book *The Richest Man in Babylon* by George S. Clason.

In the book, one of the foundational pieces of advice is to save 10 percent of your income. If I had that knowledge back then, I would have followed this advice and not only saved the 10 percent but would have created an account with a bank or credit union that I normally don't bank with.

For example, I'm sure you have heard of USAA, and you might even bank there. I started an account with them just a few short years after enlisting and have been with them ever since. I would find another bank—let's say Chase, for example—set up an account with them, then set up automatic payments to go into that account. Never look at it, and live off of what you're making without it.

After every pay raise, including any bonus pay such as flight pay, I would increase the savings to the point of my current standard of living that I was comfortable with. Comfort creep happens to all of us. We get a pay raise, we tell ourselves we need that new sofa, or that subscription, or twenty Xbox games, and it all adds up.

If you live within your means, which I completely admit is easier said than done, you can start to acquire true wealth. There are so many things you can do with your money, and buying that sports car probably isn't it.

The best time to start is when you're young. The second-best time is now. Save your money, then invest it in real estate, commodities (such as gold and silver, and now crypto currencies like Bitcoin), stocks, or business. At the very least, use a savings account, but know that the interest you typically get back with a savings account doesn't even cover inflation. You almost pay the bank to keep your money in the account.

When I was young, there was little in education on money management. There were some actual books, but they were expensive, took up space, and were sometimes hard to find. Today you can just jump on Google or Amazon, and in seconds, boom, you can see reviews, download the book, and start reading.

Educating yourself on money and finances is one of the most important self-improvement steps you can take for yourself. If I knew then what I know now, I would have bought a house at every duty station, made some improvements, then rented it out after the move. It sounds stressful, and it is; however, with today's number of property managers and the wealth of online resources, it's nearly a can't-miss strategy. As a military member, you also have great advantages, such as utilizing a VA loan, that others don't have.

With a VA loan, you can purchase a house with zero down. They add the closing costs and fees to the mortgage, and you don't even have to worry about it. Then when you move locations, you do it again.

There are specific rules you will need to follow on how many VA loans you can have and what qualifies, so do your research. I'm not telling you this is what you should do; it's what I would do if I were starting over again. A few fellow members I know have increased their assets and net worth this way, plus having a little extra money coming in every month always helps.

Lastly, there is so much free knowledge on the internet. Seek it out. If you don't know or understand something, research it. I guarantee you can find someone who has done what you're looking to do. On the flip

side of the equation, inevitably, there will come a time when you re-enlist, extend your term, or sign up for some retention bonus research as well. In addition, if you deploy, move to a new location, or live overseas, your pay will change, so make sure you stay on top of all the changes.

This comes down to watching out for yourself, because if there is a mistake and you're being overpaid, it will be found out. And not only that, but they will take it all back at once. I had my last paycheck completely taken from me for such a situation, which kind of sucks when you are expecting over $4,000 and you get nothing.

So remember to stay on top of it both ways, as you might be entitled to some pay that was missed. I would frequently see this during a move. We would go from a cheaper living location to a more expensive location where my Basic Allowance for Housing (BAH) would drastically increase, and it would be missed. I had to submit additional paperwork to get it corrected, and then they would back pay me for the time it was missed. Living in Washington, DC, is pretty challenging with a BAH of Spokane, Washington.

Don't you know my husband's a colonel?

Just as important as your health and well-being is that of your family. Throughout your career you will ask your spouse and children to endure long days without you. In addition, there will be the constant moving, changing jobs, and trying to find new friends. This can take a toll on your family, and in order to make it work, you have to help make them resilient. How do you do this? Well, some of it will be by being social.

My first wife couldn't handle Minot. She didn't have a job and was home most of the time. This led to boredom and shopping, both of which don't amount to much good. Luckily, Amazon really wasn't a thing yet. In order for her to have had a better time, I should have introduced her to the other spouses, attended more events, hosted gatherings, and potentially had her pursue a job. If you're a religious person, find a local church, as this can be a great way to find a community to belong to. Life was much better when the unit was doing things together and the spouses were always included.

I joke all the time about my time at Minot and how the climate changed drastically as different things happened. When I had arrived, times were good, but then an event triggered the dark ages. It took some time, but eventually the unit morale improved, ushering in the renaissance.

Prior to the renaissance, nobody really sponsored events or had people over. If this is happening, motivate your spouse to get out and start inviting the unit spouses over. Ensure they know about all the programs designed to help out military spouses. Have them sign up to Facebook military spouse groups. Set up plans for if and when you deploy, which could be as simple as having your spouse and the kids move back to their hometown. Staying local (on or near base) is usually the best solution, though, because other military spouses know exactly what they will be going through.

Make sure your will is up to date at all times and that you have set up who will have power of attorney for you. It's never fun trying to gain access to something while your spouse is halfway around the world. There are also events held on base, local community events, and more to help military spouses quickly adapt to their ever-changing environments.

In addition, communicate, communicate, communicate. Talk about your job, explain the endless acronyms, and make your spouse ask you to stop talking. The more transparent you are, the more you can use each other as times get tough, and they will. Hopefully the tough times don't last for too long, but be ready, as issues always tend to pop up. Organizations can change hands, and this can move people to another base at a moment's notice, so talk about the stress your spouse might be feeling.

The last item on this subject I would like to address is rank. You will hear of this (and it's a real thing): some spouses use their husband's/wife's rank as if it were their own. Don't let your spouse be "that girl or guy." They do not have the same rank as you, and make sure they understand that. The longer you are in the military, the more they will feel they are part of it too, but don't let them step it up to that next level.

Blood money and the consequences

I was reaching the end of my contract as a pilot. I had incurred a ten-year commitment, which began once I received my pilot wings. It had taken about two years to complete pilot training, then I had another three years of enlisted time, so that actually totaled fifteen years.

At the time there was a pilot shortage, and the Air Force was offering a pilot bonus. This would lock me into another five-year commitment, and I would receive a bonus paycheck for every year I owed to the Air Force. Remember that because it will be important later.

I looked at my options with my flight experience. I was primed to get a good civilian pilot job, so that was on the table. On the other side, the extra five years would take me to twenty years and full retirement. As a matter of fact, the commitment would expire two months prior to hitting twenty.

I weighed my options, and while I was frustrated in my current job, I decided retirement was worth it, not to mention the bonus that would be used to pay down some bills. Had I been smarter when I was younger, I would have invested all of it. As it was, I used a large majority of it to pay down debt. I had made my decision that when I hit my commitment and was offered the bonus, I would take the blood money.

I patiently anticipated the date when the bonus would be offered to me. My last commitment in the Air Force was exciting stuff. Then sequestration hit:

Budget sequestration is a provision of United States law that causes an across-the-board reduction in certain kinds of spending included in the federal budget. Sequestration involves setting a hard cap on the amount of government spending within broadly defined categories; if Congress enacts annual appropriations legislation that exceeds these caps, an across-the-board spending cut is automatically imposed on these categories, affecting all departments and programs by an equal percentage. The amount exceeding the budget limit is held back by the Treasury and not transferred to the agencies specified in the appropriation bills.

-Budget sequestration definition from Wikipedia, the free encyclopedia

I watched the news, asked finance about the status of the bonus, got updates from our commander on the current status of the government, and I waited. The Special and Incentive Pay Office informed me that more than likely the bonus would come back, but they just didn't know. I took the gamble that the bonus would come back and stayed in.

Then:
In December 2013, the Bipartisan Budget Act of 2013 increased the sequestration caps for fiscal years 2014 and 2015 by $45 billion and $18 billion, respectively, in return for extending the imposition of the cuts to mandatory spending into 2022 and 2023, and miscellaneous savings elsewhere in the budget.

Still no word on whether the aviation retention bonus was going to be offered again. My April date on which I would hit fifteen years was rapidly approaching, and I needed to decide a course of action. I had already decided to finish my twenty years, but I still wondered if I would get a bonus like the rest of my peers. April 14 came and went, and I continually checked to see if the bonus was offered again.

Finally, in June it was offered. I received an email and replied as quickly as I could to sign up. I finished all the paperwork the next day and awaited approval. It took another month, then was finally approved on July 1.

Crap, this would take me past my twenty years, but that was ok. I would just extend the extra few months. No harm, no foul. I could do the extra time. Now fast-forward to April 2019. I was within a year of retirement and was sent a form to fill out stating whether I would like to extend past twenty years or not. Not thinking anything of it, and knowing it would be just a little over twenty years, I elected to do that.

The years flew by, and I was then sent an email informing me I was within a year of retiring and needed to set a date. I requested July 1, which would take me a few months over twenty years. I wouldn't have an issue with my bonus, and besides, I had a five-year commitment from when I signed the paperwork. While this was less than ideal, I had planned on honoring it.

My requested retirement date was rejected.

I was very confused. How could they reject my retirement date? It didn't make sense. Along with the rejection notice was a reference to retirement regulations. Turns out you can only extend up to the first day of the month after the date you hit twenty years. This meant I was being forced to retire on May 1, which kind of freaked me out. What about my bonus?

I called Retirements, and they said that the retirement superseded the service commitment and would have to be honored. I would have to repay two months of bonus pay. When I asked what I could do, they provided me with information to request a waiver to not pay back the bonus. I submitted the waiver and then received notification that my retirement had been approved.

In the retirement package it stated there was a waiver, and the appropriate documents were present. In my view this meant the waiver had been approved, and I went on my merry way. My retirement came and went, then I noticed I never received my last paycheck. After visiting finance a few times, I finally found out that my unused retention bonus was taken from my final paycheck—which essentially was all of it. I began the process of submitting more documents and more waivers.

I thought I had been on top of it, but the waiver and the retirement were two separate things. Only the retirement was approved, and the waiver was never sent up to the appropriate approving official. In the end my service was worth it, but I was still frustrated with the system.

The Air Force provided so much invaluable training and helped me develop into a well-rounded individual. I highlight this to impress upon you to take care of yourself and be proactive. Make informed decisions and find out all the facts. There were multiple layers that I didn't understand, and I didn't know the full repercussions of signing a certain document.

In hindsight I should have asked to extend past twenty years and then requested to retire July 1. The military has rigid rules, so be your own lawyer, or ask the correct people questions to ensure you know that what you're doing is correct. I had not talked to the right people at first, and it ended up costing me time and, in this case, hard-earned money.

Decisions for taking blood money

In my career I shot some rounds in my foot. Not actually, but figuratively. I had made the conscious effort to forgo the box checking and all but ensure I would not be promoted higher than major.

For me that worked out, but I was often asked why I didn't just check the box to get my masters, and finish ACSC online. My response was usually along the lines of telling people I wanted to fly. Making lieutenant colonel would inevitably reduce that and force me into more of an office role. I wasn't really looking for that. This comment was usually met with, "You could still fly, and you would get paid more." While that statement for me was technically true, it was only in the short term.

Sure, I would have made more money when I pinned on the rank, but retirement, nope, it's high three. What does that mean? It means that the highest rank I held for a minimum of three years would be my retirement pay (well, half of the base pay). In order for me to be eligible to retire as a lieutenant colonel, provided I made it in the zone, I would have to add an additional year to my commitment. At this point money wasn't as great of a draw as it had been in the past.

We have to make educated decisions based on what we want and what is best for us. You will have to do the same. Not everyone aspires to stay twenty years. My best friend did fifteen then separated and is doing quite well. He had personal goals outside the military, and the sooner he was able to start them the better. He is not regretting it, but he also learned so much from the Air Force as well.

While the government retirement paycheck is nothing to scoff at, his quality of life is more aligned with his personality. On the other end of the spectrum, I have another friend who decided to take the bonus. He was money driven and that really influenced his decision. He signed the paperwork almost reluctantly. Then, as the civilian pilot job market heated up, he has regretted it. With his skills, he could have been making a lot of money in the civilian world and, if he invested the extra income correctly, would have a nest egg to rival the military pension.

At the end of the day, it will be your choice. You will leave the Air Force

either on your own accord or when they force you out. Even "lifers" will eventually leave. Pick your time to go, and don't let anyone else choose for you. Make a well-informed decision, and don't regret it. Not everyone has the honor of serving in the military.

G's lessons learned

Family and friends are one of the most important parts of everyone's lives. Without them we are lost, lonely, and unmotivated.

So, what do you do with an invaluable asset? You take care of it, and one of the best ways to take care of your family is money. I know it's a touchy subject, and while some people will say it doesn't drive them, it does. Without it you can't survive; you can't feed your family or give them somewhere to live. Make sure that you are adding them into the equation when making decisions about your career.

This may change over time. Remember, I chose to finish my career at twenty years and have enjoyed the extra time with my family. I could have taken another bonus and stayed in, but my family time was more important to me.

Just remember *ohana.*

CHAPTER SIX: ARTICULATION

Articulation *- the action of putting into words an idea or feeling of a specified type. plural noun: articulations "it would involve the articulation of a theory of the just war"*

This chapter covers a very important topic to everyday-life communication. This is key for success as an airman and in life, as a misunderstanding can destroy a great plan or relationship.

Questions to ask yourself:

- Question 1: How well do you communicate? Are you frequently misunderstood? If so, how can you change that?
- Question 2: When in a stressful environment do you freeze or talk incoherently?
- Question 3: Email and written communication are important for an airman. How well do you write?

What did you say?

The hottest skill in the world. Some have it, some don't, some learn it, some won't. It's the most important yet underestimated skill in the United States Air Force: communication.

You could write multiple books on the subject, and guess what? People have. One of the biggest failures in the Air Force in my opinion is communication. Nine out of ten failures of a task I could chalk up to miscommunication. If you can only enhance one skill, I would recommend communication.

Having two young boys, I have learned a lot about nonverbal clues. We communicate with much more than our words, and through my children I see this all the time. Occasionally, my five-year-old will try and use sign language to ask for things, and I find myself saying, "Use your words."

Sometimes I feel like this in the office. People try to communicate something, and I feel like I'm on a different planet trying to translate. I would find myself hesitant to ask what they meant for fear of looking

stupid. I always found it better to ask sooner rather than later, because you usually can get away with it since people are excited to sound smart, and you will get on their good side.

Bonus: I could always use the crutch of saying I'm Polish too, which was my get-out-of-jail-free card.

If you want a good book on communication, I would recommend *How to Win Friends and Influence People* by Dale Carnegie. There's a lot of good stuff in it. The biggest issue is we all deliver and interpret information differently. We are thinking of a response before people are done talking, and we say phrases we understand but the listener might not. Adding on to that, we talk in acronyms, which differ depending on the context where the acronym is used.

Here is my advice on communication: know your audience, speak in terms your audience knows, don't just hear what someone is telling you but really listen, ask questions, and follow up.

Listen, don't just hear

This one is the hardest thing to accomplish. We all have so much going on in our lives, and often I find my mind wandering: maybe it's a project I'm working on, what's for dinner, or, wow, that sky is really blue.

Listening takes a lot of patience. We are very self-centered individuals, and in today's society everyone is looking to give their input. One of the biggest problems we face today is building up what we want to say in our minds.

I find myself doing this quite frequently. I will key off on something someone says, it will trigger in my brain something I want to bring up or say, and I miss the whole conversation after that. I find myself starting to talk and at the same time thinking, "What else did they say?"

Be patient, wait your turn to speak, and ask open-ended questions to get the other person to detail things more clearly. I know it's easier said than done, but it's very true, and just like learning a new skill, you will not be a professional overnight.

Listening takes practice and, more importantly, patience. In today's society everyone wants everything now, and our attention spans have diminished. This combination makes listening even more important, and you will excel in whatever you do by honing your listening skills.

Know your audience and speak in terms your audience knows

If you are communicating with your peers and they understand text-speak, then by all means have at it. But if you're talking to your supervisor, break it down into the language they understand.

I knew I was getting old when I had a young lieutenant text-speak an entire sentence. I had no idea what she was talking about and had to figure it out. If you're talking to tech support, then you're going to have to be more technical to get through the conversation quicker. (Remember, always try a reboot of the system before anything else.)

Recently, I have been breaking things down into simple descriptions. When I do ask an individual if they know anything on the subject, I always make sure they know I don't want to insult their intelligence. If they know the subject, then I spring back into terms they would understand; if not, I would simplify my language.

Send. . . . "Oh crap, I didn't want to send that!"

There's nothing worse than typing up an email, getting ahead of yourself, clicking send, then as it's riding off to cyberspace, noticing the verbiage probably isn't going to convey your message correctly. Unlike verbal communication, it can be difficult to convey true meaning with email. Caps Lock may scream, "DO IT NOW," when what you really meant is "It's a high priority," without an angry tone.

When typing emails, remember to proofread, proofread, proofread. I have sent plenty of emails where, after looking at the response, I realized I misspelled words, my message was misunderstood or, of course, I forgot the attachment. Without other cues, text can have multiple meanings. A harmless email meant to ask a simple question may come across as an attack.

I believe one underutilized solution to this is the phone. You can figure out the message much better over the phone as opposed to just words on the screen. Most people will associate with you as a person if they hear your voice, instead of some robot on the other end of the Ethernet cable. This will help with getting the point across or the question asked in the proper tone. If you have a very technical question, or need clarification, I recommend you just pick up the phone and call.

Another thing to do, especially if you are angry and feel like writing an attack email, is to take some time to calm down. I recommend overnight. If an issue needs an immediate response, have someone else proofread your email and see what they think. An outsider will give you an unbiased opinion and help you understand what the message conveys to them.

Most issues don't need to be resolved immediately, and there have been plenty of times I have written an email in a fit of rage, then my better sense prevailed. I deleted it and attempted it the following day or even a few hours later, after I had a chance to really think about the situation.

Overall, I would recommend, if you can, to get out of your chair and go talk to the person, then follow up with an email reminding them what you talked about. If that is impractical, then use the phone or leave a voicemail. The final thought should be email, but too often it's our first go-to.

I also would recommend using some sort of note-taking app on your phone. My wife still uses a pen and paper notepad, which I have read is a proven tactic even in today's high-tech world.

I always hated it when someone would ask me to send them an email to remind them of what we had talked about. It always made me feel like they were lazy. I caught myself almost doing the same thing a few times but managed to jot down some notes or put it in my phone, and then I would start the email chain.

Ask questions and follow up

This is probably one of the most misunderstood parts of communication, and some of it goes back to the audience. When I say ask questions, there are two types in reference to a task. The first is directed back at the individual giving you the task, and these questions should be concerning the big picture.

For example, if I ask you for a spreadsheet of the quarterly ammo expenditures, an appropriate question would be: "Would you like it broken down between normal and tracer rounds?" An inappropriate question would be: "How do I create a spreadsheet?" This question is asking for help, not actually providing details for the solution. Remember, you can find a lot of those types of answers on YouTube. If you don't know how to do a part of the task, find a peer who has done it and is savvy at the task.

Next, always ask for the deadline. This will motivate you to finish on time and also help your supervisor to remember to check up on the project. I have seen that missed too many times because people get sidetracked and don't finish the task by the time the supervisor expects it to be done. A good supervisor will provide you with a deadline, but sometimes they forget.

The final part is the follow-up. Along the way of accomplishing the task, follow up with your supervisor to see if the direction you are heading is the way your supervisor asked for it. If it's not, redirect. In all cases, following up will show your supervisor you're actually working on the task. One minor note: When asking for the follow up, don't come across as "Look at me—look what I'm doing."

G's lessons learned

Communication is one of the most important things in life. In Malcolm Gladwell's book *Talking to Strangers,* he details how misunderstandings led to the fall of the Aztec empire due to the misinterpreted language with Cortez.

While we will typically be speaking the same language, we all have a slightly different way of communicating. This can be very evident in email and other written communication where visual cues are not there. As humans, we pick up on visual cues and body language almost more than what is actually spoken.

Be careful when writing emails, and when in person, be sure you are conveying the right message with your body language. We have all seen the briefer who is monotone and not into the presentation, so it's difficult to get through it, or the supervisor who tasks you with one thing and you accomplish it, only to have to redo it because they meant something totally different.

The devil is in the details.

CHAPTER SEVEN: IDENTITY

Identity - *the characteristics determining who or what a person or thing is. ["attempts to define a distinct Canadian identity"]*

This chapter covers how your character and the decisions you make will shape your future in the Air Force and throughout life.

Questions to ask yourself:

- Question 1: Do you know what you are good at and how to apply it to your job?
- Question 2: What kind of character do you have? Can you think of both good and bad examples?
- Question 3: Are you humble, and do you understand when there is a time to follow and a time to speak up?

Gears of a clock

One of my favorite animated movies is *The Incredibles*. During one scene, after helping an old lady navigate the maze of insurance claims to receive her much-deserved money, Mr. Incredible is called into his boss's office.

While in the office, his boss (whom you come to despise within seconds) starts to describe the company as a clock, each gear meshing with another in a perfect fitting order. While I'm not here to tell you to mindlessly be a gear in the clock, you need to be the best at your job that you can be.

Regardless of how your career goes, you will always have a choice to continue down your path or change career fields. If you are not enjoying or not good at your current job and see someone doing something you think you could do, do it! There will be obstacles, but they can be overcome.

For instance, once you are selected to an airframe as a pilot, it can be difficult to nearly impossible to switch aircraft. I've seen it done before, though. The Air Force spends so much money training pilots that it isn't worth it to have pilots change. Gone are the days when a pilot would be authorized to fly multiple types of aircraft.

On the enlisted side, I have seen career fields with low manning numbers make it nearly impossible to cross train. Notice I said nearly. I have seen it done. We all have a role to play, and if one individual isn't pulling their weight, it slows down all the gears. If you have peers slowing down the gear, help them speed it up.

I was trained to be an electronic warfare technician. I wasn't a jet mechanic. Had I wanted to be a jet mechanic, I could have crossed trained, but I was fine with my job, so I did it the best I could, and it opened up opportunities for me.

Working on ECM pods while most of my peers took shortcuts, I studied the systems to get a better knowledge of the inner workings and was able to troubleshoot better than most. The crew chiefs would make fun of my career field and say we were "card pullers," because nine out of ten times when a test failed, we would remove and replace one or more of the over fifty-two circuit cards in the ECM pod.

I resented the name tag and thought it was funny because the crew chiefs would do the same thing except with boxes. Being kind of a nerd (yes, I self-admit I'm part nerd) I continued to get better at finding and fixing other issues that eventually would manifest themselves in the cards.

There was one pod that sat on the test station for over a month. After looking through diagram after diagram, I had isolated it down to one cannon plug. For those who don't know, a cannon plug is a mass of electrical wires that could be disconnected from another section and sometimes would get corroded and wouldn't conduct the signals properly. I had tested the plug multiple times and with our test equipment tested the pulses that were flowing through the plug.

After going back and forth between the schematic and the plug outputs, I determined the schematic was mislabeled. Two of the wires were backwards. I checked a few other pods and they were all miswired according to the schematic. Somewhere along the way the troubleshooting book was printed in error, but due to that plug rarely going bad, the issue had never arisen. This plug had been rewired by the schematic and was sending the wrong signals. I rewired the plug and, sure enough, that fixed it.

As a gear in the clock, I was spinning and doing my part and doing it the best I could. As you progress, do your best to be a fully functioning gear. For me this led to being selected to a special test team and allowed me opportunities others didn't receive.

Throughout my career, I continued to do the best I could at each job I had. Now, I will be honest with you: there were some times I was less than stellar and started to drag my feet, but there was always a wakeup call that motivated me to step up my game. There will be times where you think that your job sucks, and maybe it does, but there is always something worse.

Believe it or not, there was a time while flying helicopters at Minot where I thought it was the worst job in the Air Force. We were under a lot of stress, lots of inspections, extra pressure from the commander, extra tests for the seemingly unending inspections. There was a drinking incident, which completely killed morale and created an overly businesslike atmosphere in the unit. I was going through a rough time with my wife, who eventually left for California. Life sucked. Or so was my thinking.

Then I thought about it more. Did life suck or was I living in the world I was building? While testing wasn't fun, I studied more, and the tests became easier. I realized people pay thousands of dollars to fly helicopters, and, I started to push my skills and challenged myself to be a better pilot. I started spinning my gears, and the rest of the unit followed. We eventually evolved into a tight-knit unit, one in which I had some of the greatest and most memorable times.

I always feel like somebody's watching me

What you do today will not only affect you but will also teach others what is expected. I had been an instructor for a short time and the unit had developed enough that the next wave of soon-to-be instructors was about to be evaluated and sent for upgrade. One individual was a good friend whom I had flown a lot with as an aircraft commander but not as an instructor. On that day we were at the ops desk talking about different subjects, some aviation related, some not.

The topic turned to some normal copilot mistakes, and one of the topics was trim control. When flying in level flight and during the beginnings of approaches, you would ensure the aircraft was in trim to make it more efficient in the airstream. The way we determined it in the Huey was twofold.

The primary source was an instrument called a trim ball. It is a black ball that sits inside a glass tube and swings side to side based on the aircraft's position. The objective was to keep the ball centered between the two lines drawn on the glass. If the ball was right of center, you stepped on the ball or input right pedal, and the reverse was correct if it was on the left. The issue of trim control wasn't relevant just to copilots but to all pilots.

In the Huey the left seat is slightly pointed to the right, and on top of that, when you looked at the copilot's trim indicator, it would not be centered when in trim. It would be touching the right line and slightly overhang it. This caused the newbies to think they were in trim but actually weren't. This would become evident on long flights when the engineer in the back would complain about his left butt cheek hurting. There were very colorful ways that this would be conveyed to the pilots, but I'll leave it at that.

During this discussion my friend mentioned a common technique to correct trim and said he learned it from me. I hesitated and thought about it for a minute. I had never flown with him as an instructor, but he had picked it up when I was an AC. He was watching what I did when I didn't even know it.

I was instructing without ever thinking about it. People will always be watching what you're doing how you conduct yourself, even if you don't know it. It could be your commander, supervisor, or even your peers. They will pick up on things both good and bad, so I don't want you to get paranoid, but always conduct yourself like someone is watching because in reality they are.

One of the seven social sins: Knowledge without character

I've heard plenty of definitions of character. The Air Force likes to refer to it as "Integrity," one of the branch's core values. Webster's defines character

as *"the mental and moral qualities distinctive to an individual."* However, my favorite definition is from John Wooden: "Character is what you do when no one's looking."

What does this mean to you? We've all seen a poor example of this. You're working hard on something, and someone else is tasked with the same duty. As soon as a supervisor shows up, all of a sudden, your partner is working his tail off just to go back to doing nothing when the supervisor leaves.

In life you should work on your character. Remember, anything worth it takes work, and there will not always be an audience. Impress yourself; don't work hard for the praise of others. Always do the right thing, but weigh the importance of a mistake, your superior's feedback, and the consequences. Good character consists of so many things. It's helping someone out when you see them struggling; it's picking up that empty water bottle that's sitting next to the garbage can.

One of the most important things we can do in the Air Force is pick each other up. If you're on top, elevate others to where you are. Having a whole team working at a high level is key to our success. People with good character always want to lift others up. They are not the ones who are excited to see others fail. I have seen plenty of bad examples in my time, and some have risen to very high ranks, but in the end they are empty. There is something about helping others achieve their goals that fulfills the soul. You feel great and can support others.

As I progressed through my career, it was very awesome and fulfilling to see one of the pilots I had trained now excelling and kicking tail in the Air Force game. I'll talk about it a little later, but I would also step aside and attempt to give younger individuals opportunities as much as I could. I knew my goals and path were set to end at a certain point, and I wasn't going to take the limelight away from anybody if at all possible.

Work hard and help others, and it will be repaid in one facet or another. Never compromise your character, and strive to instill it in others.

Watching out for numero uno

This part may sound cynical, but there is a lot of truth to it. There will be times you need to take care of yourself, and not just in the physical sense.

The first story I would like to share with you took place just after graduating basic training when I had arrived at Keesler AFB, Mississippi, to attend my tech school. Every day we would have a formation just outside of the barracks on a large concrete marching pad. The pad was about the size of two basketball courts, and there would be close to two hundred students there in the morning. Each class would form up in a flight to march to each building which held your classes.

I was attending Allie Hall at the time, which was basic electronics. Every day was the same. The red rope, who was chosen by the Technical Instructors (TI), was a fellow student and was put in place in a leadership role to be the eyes and ears of the TI. He would begin the morning by shouting at us to "fall in."

The green ropes, also chosen by the TIs but a step under the red rope, would break us into flights, one leading each group. We stood at attention, and one of the TIs would come out and inspect us. We then began the long march to Allie Hall.

One morning I woke up and looked at the clock. You know where this is going, don't you? No, my alarm didn't go off, and no one checked on me to ensure I was up. I was only a few minutes late, but I missed the formation. I could have run to catch up, but what did I do? I gathered myself and headed over to the instructor's office.

There I waited. I was finally called in and said my reporting statement the best I could: "Airman Golembiewski reporting." The instructor looked at me and told me to speak. I informed him what had happened. In his response he was impressed that I had the integrity to self-identify my mistake and acknowledged I could have gotten away with it.

After a short talk, I was given extra cleaning duty. "Wow, welcome to the real word, kid," was all I could think about. Here I had done what I was

supposed to do and was being punished for it. I had learned my lesson and would stick this experience in the vault for a later time.

I have two points for this story, and the first is on me. Know your environment and your leadership. I should have known how strict the instructor was going to be. It was a training environment with plenty of airmen intentionally breaking rules, and they can't show any mercy for fear of others taking advantage. However, I learned that sometimes it's better to only ask for forgiveness once you have been identified.

You are going to make mistakes; we all do. I still make mistakes. We need to learn from them. In this case, I learned to never forget to triple-check my alarm and would have learned that whether or not I had admitted my guilt. All I did was make my life more difficult with the extra cleaning duty on top of the studying I already had to accomplish.

My second point goes to leadership principles. The instructor had two choices, and he chose the one that soured me on the Air Force structure. Had he given me just a verbal warning for this being my first offense, I would have learned just as much but wouldn't think twice about admitting things in the future.

The following month I was allowed to move off base because I had recently gotten married. I lived just outside the east gate, in some apartments. The squadron was a distance from the east gate so I would drive. I had my wife bring down my little red S-10 pickup truck I had in high school, and I would use that to drive to the squadron every day. It was kind of an aggressive looking thing, had a roll bar with KC lights on it and some knobby tires.

One day during formation the instructor came out in a fury. "Whose truck is that that almost ran me over?" He was pointing at mine. In my defense, I don't remember having a close call with anyone, let alone one of the TIs. Now my mind went back to what I learned. I kept my mouth shut because I knew if I admitted it was mine, nothing good would come of it, and to my knowledge I had done nothing wrong. My classmates said nothing which was a relief, as a couple of them seemed a bit shady. I guess life balances out; the TI never pursued it any further.

When I joined, there were jobs for everything, including finance, travel, and temporary duty assignment (TDY) personnel. (Yes, that's right. Someone would get orders together, arrange your air travel, and ensure you were checked into class. You would be given a packet and then off you went.)

Today is much different with automated systems. You do everything yourself. You book your tickets, you book your hotel, you follow the check-in instructions for your class. There is a lot more to do, and if you don't do it, no one will. The title of this section has a negative connotation, but I want to emphasize it not because you're selfish but because if you don't take care of yourself, no one will.

You will make mistakes, but so will others. This is usually when bad things can occur and surprise you. Here's what I mean. I'll do my best to explain it in a story.

After proving to my commander that I was ready to become an aircraft commander, I was sent to Kirtland AFB to attend aircraft commander (AC) upgrade. I began my training, but the housing for temporary students on base was full, so I was put in a hotel off base and used my government travel card, as we are instructed to do.

Halfway through training, I had to go to the finance office and submit a partial travel voucher. It was a paper product that was given to finance telling them that my unit authorized me to have temporary duty there and to pay a certain amount on my travel credit card. I submitted it, got the OK from the finance person, and thought nothing more of it.

A few months later, I completed training and headed back to Minot. A few weeks after returning, I submitted my full travel voucher requesting that finance pay off the credit card and also pay the difference for meals as was normally done. Back then this was calculated on paper; today it is all automated.

I continued about my business, then in a few days, I was called into the commander's office. I was wondering what it was for, maybe to see what I thought of training. I wasn't sure. After he called me into the office and asked me to sit down, my commander asked about my government travel

card. I told him I had filled out all the paperwork halfway through my training and completed the return paperwork as soon as I got back.

"Well, it wasn't processed and I have to give you a letter of counseling." I was shocked; I had no idea. Because I wasn't looking out for myself and assumed the paperwork had been taken care of, I was getting a Letter of Counseling (LOC). Only the bad kids got one of those.

That was a steep price to pay, but I learned my lesson, and from then on, I always did follow-up checks and made copies of all the documents I turned in. In addition, I saved all my emails in a special folder both for received and sent ones; they came in handy more than once to save my tail.

This also can come in handy for your medical issues. You should also know what's in your medical record and ensure you ask detailed questions such as a need for a waiver or additional physical therapy. When I was diagnosed with a bulging disc, I didn't think much of it since the flight doc cleared me, and I continued my flying career.

Nearly ten years later, I arrived at Andrews AFB and accomplished my in-processing. During the physical exam, I was asked if I had any medical conditions. I informed the flight doc I had a back issue that was documented in my records. "Do you have a waiver?" I was asked. I didn't have one and would have thought it was taken care of since I had been flying for ten years.

The doc left the room, and I patiently waited. She came back in after some time and told me I was grounded until I received approval for a waiver for my back issue. I was dumbfounded. I had been stationed at two separate locations for a total of ten years and no one had caught this?

It ended up costing me two more months of downtime being unable to fly and another MRI. All this happened because a waiver wasn't accomplished when I first was diagnosed with the bulging disk.

While I'm on the subject of medical, let's talk about the great features to take advantage of. For example, during pilot training I found out about a contact lens program. While I wasn't able to apply for it until I graduated

pilot training, I was chomping at the bit to get rid of my glasses. Pulling Gs with a mask is bad enough, but sweating from stress and fogging up your glasses adds challenges to an already stressful environment.

As soon as I graduated, I applied for the program and was accepted, and for the next twelve years the Air Force paid for my contacts. While this was awesome, I found out about another program approved for pilots, the PRK program, which could be best described as an alternative to LASIK. I could go into details but the basic difference is LASIK is instant but never completely heals, while PRK takes longer to work but completely heals over time.

There are lots of medical programs for you to use, so seek them out and utilize them. After the PRK, my vision was corrected to 20/15, eliminating the constant need for contacts or glasses.

While it may sound self-serving, if you aren't watching out for yourself, no one is. Take advantage of programs designed to help you along in your career, whether medical, educational, or physical. Take care of yourself!

Here's your mop

The sun beat down and it was over ninety degrees outside. Our supervisor allowed us to take off our Battle Dress Uniform (BDU) tops, which was welcomed in the hot South Carolina sun. On my knees I reached for the green weed growing out of the zero-scaped rock garden.

We had been out there for hours cleaning up the weeds, cutting back shrubs, and anything else our supervisor said needed to be done. There was a general coming for a demonstration, and we were tasked with cleaning up the grounds. I thought I had left this kind of stuff back in basic training.

There will be days you will be tasked with some less than fun jobs. The good news is they will be temporary, and the more rank you get, the fewer of those jobs you will have to do. Just remember to participate when you become a supervisor. This is where you have the opportunity to lead by example if the cards fall just right. The bad news is, no complaining. I was there too—know your role.

Later in my career I still took out trash and mopped floors, though it was much less often. I tried to lead by example when I had time to participate. However, in the beginning I had no choice, and while I grumbled (it's human nature, right?), I still accomplished the task the best I could. Just remember to be humble about it, and suck it up.

On a separate but very similar topic comes volunteer work. This is more on the enlisted side, and to be honest with you, one of the many perks of becoming an officer is to opt out of volunteering. Some of you may love to serve your community, clean up roads, volunteer at homeless shelters, and I commend you, but that just wasn't me at the time. That being said, as soon as you hit your first duty station, you will be asked to volunteer. If you want to set yourself up for success, do as much as you can handle.

When I was at my first assignment, I arrived at work awaiting the announcement. I was currently an Airman First Class (A1C), also known as the dragonfly and a two-striper. I had been working hard over the past year to ensure I knew my job well, kept my nose clean, and finished my CDCs (Career Development Courses) in record time. The typical timeline to get promoted to senior airman (SrA), a three-striper, was a little over two years. However, you could get promoted—I believe it was six months early—if you were considered to be in the top 15 percent and were awarded below the zone.

I had checked all the boxes on the package, which my supervisor had submitted for me. There were job duties, volunteer work, and a host of other categories. After waiting for a while, our commander finally arrived. This was the moment I was waiting for, and in my mind that meant six extra months of SrA pay. The commander announced the name, and thankfully I had enough sense not to pull a *Zoolander*. (I was in shock—it was Hansel.) Just kidding, but it wasn't me.

I had worked very hard and did everything that was asked of me. What was I missing? By this point in time our Component Repair Squadron (CRS) had merged with sensor operators. Their job was different than ours, but the Air Force is constantly changing and evolving as every year we are asked to do more with less.

I've seen reorganization on two scales in my career, at the squadron level and at the group level. It can lead to drastic changes, and this was no different. At the time I was a little amazed at the sensor troops and their primary job and small secondary job. Their main job required them to test the targeting pod for the F-16s. Sounds pretty legit and challenging, doesn't it? Well, except that it wasn't.

They would bring the pod in from the flight line. Actually, let me backtrack. The aircraft crew chiefs would dismount the pod from the aircraft and drive it to the sensor shop where the sensor troop would hook it up to their test equipment. Then, wait for it. . . it would pass or fail.

Pass and it went back to the flight line. Fail and they would rip it apart, solder wires, troubleshoot broken cards, fix damaged ray domes. Wait, that's what we did with our ECM pods.

Unlike what we did with our pods, the sensor troop would just ship the failed pod off to a repair station and take another working one off the rack. Yes, I'm a little sensitive to how much work they actually handled at the time, but hey, at least they cleaned the aircrew's NVGs in their spare time.

After the announcement and later that afternoon, I asked my supervisor what the new SrA did better than me. His answer was more volunteer work. From that day forward I always joked that I missed out on below the zone to Santa Clause because the airman who won had been Santa Clause at our Christmas party.

So, as you are working to set yourself apart from your peers, be Santa. I mean ensure that you are volunteering and giving back to the community in your own way. It all counts, and while I'm joking about a lot of this stuff, we need people who volunteer their time. There are a lot of great programs out there and people who need your help. So go out, work hard, keep the grumbling to yourself, and improve your unit and community.

Call a wingman

It was March in Minot. The winter still had its icy fingers on the town, but it was Friday night and we were going out. At the time the town at Minot had

the most bars per capita in all the cities in the United States, or so I was told. That night was a tradition that occurred every year in March. It was Mustache March, and to celebrate all of our hideous 'staches we would do a "bad bar tour." As a unit we would map out five to ten dive bars and hit each of them up. We would stay at each for a round or two then on to the next. Most people would identify this as a bar crawl, and plenty of college students have done the same.

Our unit was small during this time. We had only recently become a squadron, so it was easy to keep track of everybody. Plenty of shenanigans would occur, but we would always get everyone home safe. Plenty of times we would end the night at Denny's or some other breakfast location.

As you journey through the Air Force, you will find yourself at the very minimum invited to events like this or simply asked to go out for a night on the town. There is always a focus on DUIs, and it's no joke! Take care of yourself and your friends; there are so many programs out there to get you home safe with no repercussions. I personally don't drink, so I ensured everyone made it home safe, but in the absence of a teetotaler there are plenty of alternatives and no excuses. It's very easy now with Uber and Lyft, so use those things to your advantage.

If you don't want to go out, then don't. If it's not your scene, don't get pressured into it. I never felt pressured to hang out anywhere I wasn't comfortable during my whole career. Take care of yourself, and have a wingman to look out for you; they are invaluable. Also reciprocate the favor and look out for your teammates. If you don't drink, volunteer to be a designated driver. It can be pretty entertaining to be the only sober one who remembers how the story actually should be told the next day at work.

Like, like, WHAT?

I sat in the aircrew briefing room looking over the map we had planned for our sortie and the additional paperwork each flight would require. The time I had set for our brief came and went. I looked around, and while my crew was present, there was no sign of the Tactical Response Force (TRF). I raised myself from the comfy black leather office chair and headed toward the ops desk. I leaned over the desk and asked the duty desk

officer, "Hey, have you seen my TRF guys?"

"No," he responded with a puzzled look. "Let me call over and check. Maybe their schedule got messed up."

Standing there looking outside at the frozen tundra of a cold winter's day in North Dakota, I waited. It was here that I found out how addictive cigarettes truly were, as I had witnessed countless smokers brave the negative-thirty-degree temperatures in parkas and gloves to get their fix.

In the background I faintly heard the voice of the desk officer chatting on the phone, but I didn't pay much attention. I smiled when I heard a small chuckle as the phone was hung up. I half chuckled to myself. I was sure this was going to be good. The TRF had a knack for doing some entertaining things. I once watched a few of them test out Tasers on each other.

"What's up?" I asked. "Seems that the TRF are having a mandatory safety down day," he replied. I thought to myself, *That's strange. I don't remember that on the schedule.* Still smiling, the duty desk officer continued, "Turns out two of the TRF members were testing their armor-plated vests in the backyard of their house; the neighbors heard gunshots and called it in."

Now, first, to be clear, no one was injured, so don't jump to that conclusion. The funniest part of the story was the only reason they got caught was because it was within city limits and the cops were called. They had been wearing the vests and shooting each other with a shotgun.

The TRF would do lots of questionable things, and we would inevitably hear about it during our sweep flights. Where am I going with this? You guessed it—social media. Whether it's Facebook for us "old guys," Instagram, or some new thing that's not out yet, the world is watching. Your parents are watching, the government is watching, your friends are watching, and yes, your commander is watching.

With today's technology, it's more important than ever to think everything through before you do it. You are held to a higher standard as an Air Force member.
What you do not only affects yourself but your peers as well. In the past,

things would have to get crazy out of hand for leadership to "cancel Christmas." Even now, the simplest things posted in the wrong place and the wrong time could elicit a letter of counseling or even an Article 15. Be careful whom you follow, what you like/love, and groups you're a member of, any of which could land you in the commander's office.

Remember, social media is traceable, people are always recording, and even if the app tells you the message was deleted in five seconds, somebody can still take a screenshot.

Today, we live in a very visual world and need proof of everything. Take Ray Rice, for instance. He was punished for knocking out his soon-to-be wife in an elevator. Think about it; one punch and he knocked her out. That had to have been some punch. He was punished with a small penalty, and nobody thought anything more about it.

Then the video surfaced, and people were outraged. You would have thought he murdered her. The description was exactly what you see on the video, but somehow it makes it more intense to see the visual. Think about that the next time somebody wants to film you drinking fifteen shots in a minute.

It's mine, I deserve it!

"I don't know if you're struggling or if you just don't care," said my commander. This was my wake-up call. My commander had pulled me into his office to have a chat about my performance. It was early 2005 and I was a member of the 54th Helicopter Flight.

After being there for about a year, I was going through the motions. I showed up to work but didn't really do much, as my additional duty required little of me. I have found it very interesting that humans adapt to their environment very quickly, both on the good side and the bad. In my case, it was bad.

Having little to do outside of flying, and not being very happy with the local environment, I trudged along in "cruise control." This was Minot, pre oil companies, and the only chain restaurant was Applebee's. Walmart wasn't super, snow would blow through

to Minnesota, and yes, it would get to negative thirty degrees. I continued to fly and figured I would learn all I needed from that. I had stopped studying our operating manuals and figured I knew enough.

As time dragged on, I anticipated becoming an aircraft commander. It was typical at the time to upgrade to aircraft commander after being at the unit for a year. The year came and went, and I became even more disgruntled. I deserved to be an aircraft commander. It was my turn why hadn't they sent me? The commander didn't like me was what I told myself.

One morning I came in and headed to the ops desk like I did every day. The schedule was pretty simple in those days, just an Excel sheet with crew names, take off and land times, and what you were scheduled to accomplish. Everything seemed normal.

I was scheduled for a morning flight to fly a sweeps mission. On a sweeps mission you would fly around the nuclear missile complex and overfly the specific silos that were under maintenance to ensure they were secure. There was one abnormality, though. I was now scheduled with a different aircraft commander than what was on the call the prior evening. Not thinking anything of it, I prepared like any normal day. I gathered my flight gear, drew lines on a map for our flight path, then headed into the briefing room. There, my aircraft commander informed me that this would be a no-notice check ride.

In the flying community we would have a random checkout that we called a no-notice check ride. It's like the Pixar animation short called *Lifted*. If you're unfamiliar with it, you should check it out on YouTube.

I was a little caught off guard but what reduced the stress was that I was being graded to the copilot standard and would perform the sweeps mission as usual. I was given a blank, bold-faced ops limit sheet and told to fill it out prior to the flight. The boldface consisted of emergency procedures we had to memorize in case of a malfunction occurring.

Time would be invaluable and you would need to instinctively react. The operations limitations were items including oil pressure limits, airspeeds not to be exceeded, and other such items. This was less important than the boldface, and I had done very little recently to study it.

I filled out the sheet; we accomplished the brief then headed to the aircraft for the flight. The sortie went well with really no issues. Upon returning, my evaluator informed me that I would need some remedial training. At this point I was in the "whatever" mood, so I took inputs about my missed ops limits questions and went on my way.

That's when I got the wake-up call from my commander.

I had set my effort on cruise control and was just doing enough to get by. I was informed that it was my mediocre performance and lack of motivation that were holding me back from aircraft commander upgrade, and my commander was worried I wouldn't make it through the training.

I left the meeting angry. Angry against my evaluator, angry against the commander, angry against Minot and the Air Force. They didn't know my potential. I justified it in my own mind that if they sent me to school, I would do just fine. I would study when I got to Albuquerque. It was school, and I knew how to play the game.

With that in mind and no additional duties, it would be a cinch. I deserved to go to aircraft commander school. I was an excellent pilot. I didn't need to study.

After stewing on that a few days, I came to the realization that I had to prove myself. I had given my commander no reassurances in my performance that I would excel in upgrade training. I had become lazy. I was letting my environment dictate my actions, instead of me dictating them. We say all the time: fly the aircraft, don't let the aircraft fly you. I was letting the aircraft fly me and was hanging on to the tail with one hand.

Looking at it from my commander's perspective was entirely different, and I have found it a good exercise to see the other side's perspective. I began to study, I asked instructors to fly with me, I prepared for my flights better, taking everything more seriously. I was going to prove I actually deserved to be sent to AC school. I had started putting in the extra work to be a well-rounded pilot, and it wasn't long before the commander noticed that my book of knowledge had increased and sent me to aircraft commander school. Once there I was motivated to prove myself and to prove to my

commander that he had made a good decision to send me. I passed all my rides and did very well though it wasn't without a lot of effort.

At the end of the day, I got all I deserved, not because I was owed it but because I worked for it. I had deserved to be held back. I wasn't performing. Once I applied myself, I had the privilege to attend AC upgrade.

There are people out there who believe that just showing up will get them what they want. The Air Force is not like that. In order to excel and have a fun and exciting career, you have to put in the work.

If you're saying to yourself that you deserve something, think about what you have done to deserve it. If you gave nothing, you better re-evaluate your situation.

G's lessons learned

Nobody owes you anything, and you have to work for everything. This is something I learned many times and am still learning. Whenever I feel like I have "arrived," something always brings me back to Earth.

You will have plenty of jobs that suck, and while they may not be fun, when you push through them, it will be worth it. It will define your character, an invaluable and important piece of your journey through the Air Force.

People will respect you and look to offer you more opportunities if you put your head down and "shut up and color."

Working hard or hardly working?

CHAPTER EIGHT: RULES

Rule - *one of a set of explicit or understood regulations or principles governing conduct within a particular activity or sphere.* [*"the rules of the game were understood"*]

This chapter covers how the Air Force deals with its rules and regulations, how it applies to you, and how to thrive in the system.

Questions to ask yourself:

- Question 1: Do you struggle with authority? What can you do to reduce your aversion?
- Question 2: Do you understand how to read the rules, know how they apply to you, and know how to manipulate them to suit both you and the Air Force?
- Question 3: Do you know when to be professional and when to be more casual?

The Air Force game

As a captain I attended Squadron Officer School, or SOS, as it is called. We began with classes on general leadership skills, had field events, obstacle courses, and group puzzle games. One of the field events was called flicker ball. This was a made-up game, and it was designed in the image of the USAF. It was relatively simple, as game play went.

There would be two teams; each team would try to throw a dodgeball through a vertical hoop. Think basketball hoop tilted ninety degrees up, except instead of round it was square. There would be two runners under each hoop to get overthrown balls. The basic rules included tossing the ball to your teammates, but one of the tricks was they could only take one step after catching it. You would pass back and forth until you got close enough to your net to attempt a score.

Sounds simple, right? Well, in true Air Force fashion, they engineered the game to not only eliminate athleticism but to promote rule following, and the devil is in the details. The first change was well before my time. In the past, the ball used was a football, but the instructors quickly realized

games were won by athletic players who could throw the football very accurately.

The game kept evolving until it reached the game I played at SOS where the football had been changed to a small version of a dodgeball, much more susceptible to the wind and more difficult to control.

The Air Force loves its rules, and flicker ball highlighted it to a tee. I remember my class had a few athletically gifted individuals, but for many others it was not their most outstanding trait. The rules in flicker ball nearly eliminated this disadvantage, and the team that followed the rules would win.

Prior to taking the field in games, we held practices. I studied the rules and ensured my team knew them down to the simplest detail. Attention to detail was key, and one example was calling time-out. If you said "time-out" you would get a penalty because the correct term was "time." Another was that my runners under the hoop would have to yell a phrase, and only one could go get the ball. If they failed to talk or if both went after the ball, it would be a game forfeit.

I ensured they communicated well and understood these rules. I also came up with a system of passing the ball to ensure no more than one step would be taken, and I set limitations on where my team could shoot from. Needless to say, we went undefeated, not because we were better or more athletic than the other team but because we followed the rules.

The Air Force is like flicker ball. Follow the rules and you will excel. Throughout this book, I have given insight into what to watch out for and how to handle certain situations. I have a whole chapter on tips for advancing in rank and accomplishing it with minimal stress.

There will be boxes to fill, some of which need to be colored inside the lines while others just need to be scribbled in, such as college degrees. Play the Air Force game. Show up for events early, finish tasks ahead of time, play as a team. These simple tips will help you establish yourself as a solid airman.

Another example of playing the game happened to me during aircraft commander upgrade. In the helicopter pilot world of my time, you began your career as a copilot, meaning you always flew with an aircraft commander, instructor, or evaluator. It was similar to the airlines, learning from more experienced pilots, then as you increased your knowledge, judgment, and hand skills, you would attend aircraft commander school. Once you passed the upgrade, you were essentially given the keys to the car.

While cockpit resource management (CRM) played a large role in decision-making, the final authority came down to you. So, there I was after having my wake-up call with my commander and was now on my way to aircraft commander school. I arrived at Kirtland AFB New Mexico, the training hub for all Air Force helicopters at the time. There the school consisted of MH-53 Pave Lows, HH-60 Pave Hawks, and the UH-1N Hueys which I flew.

The upgrade was set up in the same manner as my initial copilot upgrade, starting with academics, then the contact phase where we executed emergency procedures, then remotes, which incorporated landing in random fields or the deserts of New Mexico, and finally tactics in which we flew at one hundred feet in a simulated threat environment. It was during this final phase that I learned a lesson about knowing my environment as well as understanding the rules and how to play them.

For normal procedures and planning purposes you would ask your instructor what to plan for the following day. My instructor simply stated, "Plan a tactical sortie like you do at Minot." I thought to myself, *Great, that's super easy.* See, our tactics at the time were to fly as fast as we could to the threat and insert our tactical response force (TRF), which was a small contingent of Air Force security forces. Simple enough, right?

The following day I arrived for the morning briefing, the weather for the day was given, the schedule was reviewed, and a few other administrative items were covered. We then broke off into our crews, and I finished preparing the briefing room for my sortie. After the entire crew arrived, I accomplished the time hack, which was a normal first step in the briefing.

For those of you who don't know what a time hack is, let me give you the CliffsNotes. The crew would put their watches in program mode, digital watch faces would flash, and analog clocks would stop. The one running the time hack would announce the time one minute in advance. For example, "In one minute the time will be 0800." You would then wait and watch the clock tick until you heard, "In ten seconds the time will be 0800." The individual would then wait and state, "Five, four, three, two, one, HACK; the time is now 0800 local."

This would all run off the Naval Observatory Master clock which the individual would have acquired by calling a phone line ahead of time and setting their watch. Today, with the internet, you can utilize many other ways to do this, and satellite clocks are updated constantly and automatically, but we still ensured the entire crew was on the same page.

After the time hack, I proceeded to start my briefing. I ensured the crew was in place, that everyone knew their assignments, and I then proceeded to address the sequence of events for the flight. In my head I was thinking that this would be a quick brief for two reasons: 1) it was very simple, and 2) my instructor had just moved from a space and missile base and knew our tactics—or so I thought.

I proceeded to show the route on the map and the landing zones I intended to utilize. This was met with confusion. Where are your turn points? Where are your alternate landing zones? Questions started pouring in. I was being assaulted, question after question, and like the plague, it became contagious, involving the other instructors in the room.

I started to argue that it was our tactics at Minot and emphasized I was told to plan like I was at my home station of Minot. "What happens if you are engaged at your primary LZ?" was asked as the hottest topic.

"I'll land farther from the threat," was my response, since that was the tactic at the time. This continued for a bit, then I realized I was the student here. I needed to get back in my role, shut up and color, and live to fight another day.

After things calmed down, we dismissed with my questionable plan and headed to the aircraft. The beginning went as planned; the route was a straight line, so navigation was a cinch. We had a few training engagements on the way where the flight engineer would announce we were being engaged by ground fire, so I would take evasive action, then we continued on our way. At the first LZ, sure enough, we were "engaged" and we had to skip the site and move on to the next.

After the sortie, I was debriefed on our tactics and what was expected of me. In the schoolhouse environment, you showed your navigation skills and tactical knowledge by planning a certain number of turn points and setting up a primary and a secondary LZ, which would be utilized if the first became compromised. I should have known better and checked with another instructor when I was told to plan "like I was at Minot."

The next sortie I was scheduled to fly with the same instructor, and now I knew what to expect. No arguing, no having my unit commander call and inform her of our tactics at Minot—I planned the sortie the schoolhouse way. The briefing went great, the sortie went even better, and I was praised for my knowledge and skill. The funny thing was I didn't fly any different, but I played the game. I had figured out what my instructor was looking for and catered my actions to that.

These are just a couple of examples of the challenges faced moving through the Air Force. Learn to play the game. There will be times when you are frustrated because you might have been taught differently or think you have a better way of doing something. There will be a time and a place for all your input.

Had I talked to my instructor and requested more information, or explained how I was being taught at Minot outside of the briefing, I would have been told the reason behind her frustration without pissing her off by looking like I was trying to get away with something. Later, when I became an instructor, I then understood her frustration, as the curriculum had a certain number of maneuvers the student has to accomplish, and if they don't, you have to incomplete or fail them.

As the Air Force evolved while I was on active duty, I witnessed plenty of change. We went from blindly following rules to questioning all of

them. Just remember nine out of ten rules are there for good reason. That one straggler probably made sense in the past, but things are changing so fast the regulations can't keep up.

Sometimes there is a reason why the monkey is getting a beatdown by the other monkeys, and other times there might not be. Know when and how to ask why. Typically, the best time is behind closed doors, but if it seems to be a sensitive subject, find someone outside your work area who might know the answer, such as someone who had a permanent change of station (PCS) or retired. If you're unfamiliar with the five monkeys story, search for it on YouTube.

If you are unable to view the video, I'll explain the premise. Scientists did a study where they put five monkeys in a cage. They then put in a ladder with bananas on top of the ladder. When one monkey climbed the ladder, the scientist would spray down the other four monkeys, so the monkeys all learned to beat down any monkey trying to climb the ladder.

The scientists then removed one monkey and replaced him with a new monkey. The new monkey would see the enticing bananas and start to climb the ladder. The fear of being doused with a wet hose would make the other four monkeys beat him down. Soon the new monkey learned not to climb the ladder.

Once they started replacing the next monkeys, the same thing would happen until none of the original monkeys were in the cage, but it continued that any new monkey would be beaten down as they attempted to climb the ladder. The monkeys had no clue of why they couldn't climb the ladder, only that they would be beaten down by the others if they did.

As the Air Force gets older and technology increases, sometimes rules need to be reviewed to understand why they are there. You may find one that is irrelevant; just make sure you ask about it through the right channels.

I love the smell of jet fuel in the morning!

It was a hot muggy summer day in South Carolina. As a hobby I had started playing paintball on the weekends. There was a wooded course

near the base, and, boy, I got way into it. I'm kind of a nerd that way; for me, it's full throttle or nothing. I not only had purchased my gear but had also made a full ghillie suit out of old BDUs netting and strips of burlap. It was pretty awesome, though. I more than once had somebody step on me without ever knowing I was there.

The owners of the field were a father and son, the latter of whom had served in the Marines. We got to know each other pretty well, as my suit was a bit of a conversation starter. We would exchange stories, and one day he told me the story of the only time he had set foot on an Air Force base.

He was deploying to some desert country, and they were using Air Force transportation to get there. They arrived on base and had some time to kill, so their superiors sent them to the chow hall to get something to eat. They were dropped off in front of the small building and headed inside. Once inside, he took a look around then turned and left because he thought that they had been dropped off at a fancy restaurant! They couldn't believe the building was a military dining facility.

This story illustrates one important fact: The Air Force has it good. I have stayed in tents with the Army while transitioning to Iraq and then arrived in country (Iraq) where AF personnel have one roommate and complain about it. The Army has multiple roommates during deployments. In the Air Force we get hotel rooms while traveling overseas; the Army gets the ground.

Once you have been active for a while and have had a chance to work with other service branches, you will quickly find out the difference. If we went into a room where everyone was dressed in civilian clothes, I could probably pick the Air Force members out of the crowd. Airmen just have different mannerisms and are cut from a different cloth.

The Air Force culture in general is quite different than that of any other service, and it's a good thing. Our missions are vastly different, and our operations tempo varies. Due to the fact that all pilots are officers instead of warrants, like in the army, this leads to a unique atmosphere that we all become comfortable in.

If you've joined the Air Force, good choice. If you're looking to join the service, you're looking in the right place.

Hi, Mom

When I enlisted, I was excited to leave home because I had a bunch of rules and curfews that were interfering with my social life. Shortly after I moved into somebody else's parent's house, however, I discovered that while I had freedoms I had never had before, such as staying out all night, I now had a full-time job with a commitment thatwould get me thrown in jail if I quit. In the Air Force, you quickly find out what you are allowed to do, where you're allowed to be, and who you can hang out with.

Having extensive time in this structure, I completely understand why they developed the rules as they have. Somebody did something stupid in the past, got injured or killed, and as a result, rules were set in place. In the flying community, there is a saying that warnings in flight manuals are written in blood, and this filters over to everything.

Some bases where I've been stationed have had location restrictions such as certain bars known to be anti-military. You will hear this a lot: the rules are written for the lowest common denominator, and as the saying goes, common sense isn't so common.

If you think big brother is watching you in the real world, that game gets stepped up in the Air Force. You have the pleasure of informing your supervisor where you are going on vacation, how long you will be there, and your mode of transportation, all of which could potentially be denied if your plan is unsafe (for example planning to drive twenty-four hours straight).

In addition, they tighten down on what you're allowed to ingest, and this is continuously being updated for fear that someone will pop positive on the drug test. This mainly becomes a factor with taking workout supplements, and having tried plenty of them myself, I've found most a waste of money.

I won't go in depth here, but studies have shown a bunch of companies put fillers and other unneeded ingredients into the supplements. This drives up cost for you, the consumer, with no added benefit.

As for drug testing, be prepared to get a random drug screening nearly every time you return from leave, and the greatest part of this is somebody gets to watch you "go." I'm guessing somebody pulled the old switcheroo like in the movie *The Program*.

While this may all seem bad, there are some rules meant to help you out. For example, they have a use-or-lose policy, and while it could become an enemy of yours, it's designed to help you keep your sanity.

The program is set up to make you take leave. Crazy, right? Who wouldn't want to take vacation? But sometimes training temporary duty, and inspections all can add up to time you are required to work, and you build up too much leave to carry forward. I never even got close to that.

There was a period when I was saving up a bunch of time, but life was so much better when I would take some time off to recharge, grow some stubble, and relax. Here is an interesting article to read if you have some time. Do a Google search for

What Vacation Does to your Body and Brain – Business insider article

The article explores the findings of vacation studies, which have determined your body gets worn down if you try to operate at maximum working capacity without taking breaks. So, take your leave!

Breaking the law! Breaking the law!

It was my last three months in Iraq. As I mentioned before, I took on my third different job as the year wore on. The group I found myself with was a small three-person team known as Joint Air Operations Integration Team, or JAOIT for short.

Our task once again was to educate the Iraqi Army about their air assets. The three of us would visit multiple locations around the country, meeting with each location's top Iraqi army general. Inevitably, we would get the same reaction. It went like this.

I would show a short video of Mi-17 helicopters flying and inserting troops, all video I had shot myself. The Mi-17s in the video, were owned

and flown by the Iraqis. This was evident by the huge Iraqi flag that was painted on the belly of the aircraft. After showing the video my first question would be, "Who owns these helicopters?" and the response would be, "The Americans." It took some time to convince them that it was their own country that owned and operated the aircraft.

We would go on to explain the US forces were leaving and that when we left the country, they would have to call their own helicopters for support. This was usually met with resistance, but eventually I believe we got our point across. At the end of training, we detailed how to contact the Mi-17 units when they required support, then it was off to the next location.

This was only one of the tasks we were assigned. Another was to integrate the Iraqi special forces with the Iraqi Air Force. To do this we were preparing the Iraqi special forces to call in an air strike on a target we placed in the middle of the desert. They would call up to a Cessna Caravan armed with a HARM missile. The special forces would give a five line over the radio, laze the target, and the Iraqi Air Force would fire the missile.

Previous to our testing, and with the help of an embedded American Spec Ops, the Iraqi special forces had been calling in air strikes with USAF air assets for over a year prior. The Iraqi Air Force had only fired missiles by themselves, never with a ground team directing the fire. This was going to be a first and was taking months to prep for and set up.

The first challenge was accomplished by some of my counterpart advisors with the Iraqi Air Force. It took some time to convince them to shoot a multimillion-dollar missile at a trailer in the middle of the desert. In the Iraqi culture, they never trained using real equipment. It was too valuable, and this included even bullets for their rifles. So I believe we promised them a replacement missile after the test.

Hurdle one done, and on to hurdle two. The trailer they were going to use as a target was what we called a CHU, or Containerized Housing Unit. It was a basic box similar to a large storage or shipping container (think PODs). We had one placed one out in the middle of the desert about a week before the testing date.

A few days later, it was gone, vanished. So once again another container was set out for the launch. Then again, it disappeared overnight. Finally, the third box was set out there and twenty-four-hour surveillance was placed on it. I think they used a predator—I'm not sure—but what they observed was local people sneaking out after dark disassembling it piece by piece and carrying it away like ants. So with the fourth box, they sent an armed escort to guard it the night before the shoot. You can't make this stuff up!

As the day neared, I was coordinating a helicopter ride for our colonel to attend the shoot from the ground. I intentionally didn't call the unit up at Taji until the day of, because I had worked with them before and understood how much pushback and chaos would ensue. I asked them if there was going to be a flight flying into Baghdad and flying out to the test site. They told me there would. I confirmed there would be an American at the set of controls, which was a rule in the country to ensure the safety of our personnel.

The plan was set. Now I had to explain to our colonel the rules for flying on an Iraqi helicopter. First it had to be a tan Mi-17, which were newly built from UAE and just purchased by the US Government. In addition to the new models, they had older models with a green paint scheme on them, and we nicknamed them "Legacy" Mi-17s. The issue we had with the "Legacy" aircraft was they were no longer being maintained to American standards.

As we cut funding, we pulled back support on a lot of fronts, and this was one of them. In the past, the Iraqis had purchased non-airworthy parts to repair their aircraft, and we were worried that this would happen again. I made sure the colonel understood the difference.

Second, there had to be an American pilot at the set of controls for another American to fly as a passenger. This was for obvious reasons; there had been a few crashes due to the Iraqi pilots making some poor decisions, so leadership was taking every precaution they could to ensure our safety. He acknowledged that as well.

Shortly after the discussion, the colonel left for the helipad. I stayed in the office to man the phone, and soon after the scheduled departure, I

received a call from an army colonel who sounded less than pleased. He asked if the flight had left for the test site, and I told him I had no way of knowing but according to the schedule it did. He informed me the Army sergeant whom my colonel had taken with him was unauthorized to fly on an Iraqi helicopter. This was a point of contention with the Army and one of the reasons I was there as an Air Force officer working with Iraqi helicopter units.

Let's travel back in time to when the US Government decided to support the rebuild of the Iraqi forces. The Army was asked to support the helicopter buildup, and this completely made sense due to the US Army having over 5,000 helicopters and the US Air Force having less than 1,000. I don't know the specifics, but I was told the Army wanted nothing to do with it due to airworthiness concerns. What happened?

The Air Force stepped up and said they would work as advisors for the Iraqi helicopters. They believed this made sense because under the new structure we were teaching them. All Iraqi air assets would be lumped under the Iraqi Air Force. This lasted until about three months after I arrived when the Iraqis elected to split off the helicopters into their own command, but that's another story.

Back to the current one, I did my best and immediately called the LZ controller, and sure enough, they had already left. I asked for the description of the Mi-17s, and the controller informed me they were both a green camouflage color. I called the colonel back and he informed me not to let his troop get back on the helicopter. I told him I'd do my best, but I had no way to contact them and that was the truth.

The day continued on, the test fire time came and went, and then my colonel showed up. As soon as he came in, you could tell exactly what his background was. "It was awesome," he stated. "Stuff went flying everywhere, and they destroyed the target." He was an F-16 pilot by trade, and you could tell he had always loved his job.

After he settled down, I calmly asked him, "How was the helicopter flight?"

"Great. It was better than driving," he replied.

"What color was it?" my next question popped out. "Green," he said without even flinching.

"Was there a US pilot up front?" I asked, already knowing our pilots were unauthorized at the time to fly on the "Legacy" MI-17s.

"No."

"So did the army guy fly back with you?"

"No, some of the ground guys said he had to stay there."

"Good," I responded. Then I told him about the angry army colonel who called explaining his frustration with the travel situation and the hazards of flying with the Iraqis.

Apparently, they sent a ground convoy out to go pick up the colonel, and it was going to take some ridiculous time to get there, like a two-hour drive. The flight was only thirty minutes. By this time, it was almost 2011 and there were extra rules set in place for safety.

All the top brass was worried about casualties, and everything became very restricted, making it nearly impossible to accomplish our goals at the tactical level. Big picture: if we didn't train the Iraqis before we left, they would train themselves, or worse, not train at all. I wanted to do my part to help them attain success so we wouldn't have to be there much longer or go back again later.

That day I had bent and ignored some of the rules to accomplish the mission and so had my colonel. It was a first for the Iraqi military, and now they had the confidence to do it. I learned what good leadership was that day, not only accepting the correct level of risk but also covering for your troops.

The general in charge of us was assaulted by the army generals about us breaking the rules, but I had only heard that from his staff. He never came down on us and actually thanked us for the mission success. The previous general would not have done that. There will be times when you may have to bend or break/bend the rules, but you can't just

arbitrarily do it. Take in all the facts, especially if lives will be on the line, and trust me, they will.

At this point in time, the Iraqi helicopter pilots had been trained well. They were trained by some outstanding instructors, many of whom I had flown with. I talked with them and was impressed by the success they had. The red tape we would have gone through to schedule the flight would have taken months and more than likely the flight would have been denied, so I made an educated decision to complete the mission.

The rules are there for a reason, especially in the flying community, but we also have a statement established in our regulations that if it's in the judgment of the aircraft commander to accomplish the mission or for the safety of flight, we are allowed to deviate from the rules. That is what separated us from the Russians during our past conflicts and something you must learn to do to succeed in the Air Force.

Two knights faced each other

A few months before I retired, there was a big event for the missileers in Cheyenne. I drove out to the large missile maintenance bay on the north side of the base. Cars were everywhere, and the closest parking spot was about a quarter mile away. I climbed out of my truck, donned my hat, and walked down the long road toward the event.

As I approached the main parking lot, there was an airman standing on the corner. I greeted him and he responded with, "Hey." Being a little in shock and not necessarily a confrontational person, I continued my walk to the event wondering if the rank on my hat and chest was missing.

In my last few years, this lack of respect occurred more than a few times, including many instances such as this day where there was no salute. Remember your customs and courtesies at all times. There's a reason we teach, "When in doubt, whip it out." I should have been saluted, and I hope that when the major passed this airman, he saluted. Not all officers are as easygoing as myself.

In hindsight I should have mentioned something to him in private. There are rules, structure, and tradition for a reason. As I made my way through my career, I can't say I necessarily loved saluting, but I did it out of respect and tradition, which are there for a reason.

That individual you are saluting has more experience and has put in more work than you. There is a scene in *Band of Brothers* where Major Winters walks past his old training instructor Captain Sobel whom Winters has passed in rank. Captain Sobel is reluctant to salute, but Major Winters reminds him he is saluting the rank, not the man.

In addition, traditions are fun and make us unique. You don't see businessmen have those traditions, and I have seen USAF traditions all but disappear through my career. I have an extensive patch and coin collection. These things were traded extensively in the past, but the closer I edged to retirement, the less and less I found anyone who even knew what a coin challenge was—and it's not something you only play in Vegas or on your phone.

These issues filtered over to normal Air Force etiquette. For example, while it's human nature to treat people you've known for a long time as a friend, if they are your superior, you still need the "Sir" and "Ma'am" in there.

"What's up?" is not the greeting you should be giving your commander. Professionalism is very important, and you will be judged on it. The next time a good deal or award comes along, guess who will more than likely miss out: the unprofessional airman.

There is also something I have heard plenty of times through my career, especially in the flying community I was in. We would have some flight engineers who would make comments that they could have been a pilot but didn't want to, or could have done all these better things with their life. Don't be that person.

If you can do something great, go out and do it. If you think that you deserve to be respected like an officer or the next rank up, go out and earn it, as there are more than enough opportunities out there.

And I have a secret for you; it's not hard; it just takes effort. If effort is hard for you, then I'm sorry but you're not going to be able to excel. Yet I guarantee you can!

G's lessons learned

Rules are meant to be followed. Some have been around long before you were born, and some are evolving as the world changes. While you should follow the rules, you need not blindly follow them. Initially, you should follow them, but as your knowledge increases, you can begin to ask why.

If you do ask why and are shut down, either it's too complicated to explain in the amount of time allotted, or the person you asked is just one of the monkeys who doesn't know why.

Sometimes you need to find out, so climb the ladder and maybe you won't be hosed down.

CHAPTER NINE: MOTIVATION

Motivation - *the reason or reasons one has for acting or behaving in a particular way.*
["escape can be a strong motivation for travel"]

This chapter covers one of the most important and difficult topics to teach. Everyone has different motivations and drive. In this chapter I will demonstrate how my determination and motivation propelled me through an entire Air Force career.

Questions to ask yourself:

- Question 1: What motivates you?
- Question 2: Are you a self-starter, or do you need a little push?
- Question 3: When things become difficult, how do you respond?

Grit

Webster defines grit as firmness of mind or spirit: unyielding courage in the face of hardship or danger.

Of all the topics I cover in this book, I believe this is the most important. My hopes are that you take this as a seed and grow it. If you take only one thing from this book, I want it to be this. It's not something you are necessarily born with, you can't buy it, you can't trade for it, but you *can* acquire it. Grit.

There are plenty of examples in history of people who have been beaten down and then risen up to the challenge. Maybe they just needed some words of inspiration, a friendly helping hand, or even just a "job well done" for a small task performed. Grit was something that was instilled in me when I was young, but I had to cultivate and grow it through the years.

There were days I struggled with a problem and knew that giving up would be an easy solution. But is it the right solution? Should I have just thrown in the towel when I struggled in pilot training? It would have been easier, sure, but my perseverance allowed me to find and do something I love, flying, not to mention I never would have met my awesome wife without it.

I remember at one time my goal was to use my electronics background to work at Chuck E. Cheese fixing arcade games. I can't imagine doing that now as a full-time job.

Perseverance: it's in your mind—no one can take it from you, but you can give it away. In an article in *Parenting Magazine* written in 2005, grit was found to be the number one factor in what a child becomes. This quote from Angela Lee Duckworth, a University of Pennsylvania psychologist, sums it up:

"The most significant predictor of success in kids isn't social intelligence, good looks, physical health or IQ. It's about having stamina, sticking with your future—day in, day out, not just for the week, not just for the month, but for years—and working really hard to make that future a reality."

Continue to persevere, to work on your craft, your skill, or your job. We're not born able to do everything. We learn it. For some of us it comes harder than others, but put in the time and it will come to you. As I struggled with pilot training, I just kept plugging away, studying, working hard, getting better each time. Maybe it was only a little each time, but it was in the right direction.

As a commander I have assigned people tasks, and I would see them give up or in some extreme cases never get started. This made it difficult to accomplish our goals as a unit. It meant I had to search for another individual, which then ate up my time or, in some cases with a tight time window, had me doing the task myself. If you are given a task and it's difficult, find a solution, find help, ask for clarification, and use your grit.

In life in general, I find the hardest thing to do is get started. One of my softball teammates in DC would always say, referring to scoring a run at the beginning of the game, "The first one's the hardest." And he is right! I have thought of starting many projects and was frozen with fear to begin. Thoughts would go through my head, including, "What if I mess it up?" I was afraid of failure, or messing things up so badly it could lose me time, money, and sometimes face.

One good example is the kit car project I worked on. At the time I was stationed at Fairchild AFB in Spokane where I had a 1977 Jeep CJ-7 that

my friend and I had taken down to the frame and fully restored. It was sweet! Fiberglass body, a Chevy 350 we had rebuilt from scratch, and big Super Swamper tires. It was a beast.

After my tour in Iraq, I decided to take my wife to Silver Lake Sand Dunes in Michigan. I had stored both my one-and-a-half-ton Chevy Kodiak and the restored Jeep at my parents' house during the deployment, and I arrived there ready to drive my stuff to Spokane. Our plan was to drive up the west coast of Michigan through the Upper Peninsula, kayak at the painted rocks on Lake Superior, and then continue the long journey to Spokane.

After the first day of traveling, we arrived at Silver Lake. No sooner were we on the dunes than I blew out the rear differential. This put a damper on the enjoyment of actually taking out the Jeep for the first time since the build. We packed it back on the trailer then made the multiple-day drive home. It then sat in our barn for the next two years collecting dust. Time had gotten away from me and I had found things I enjoyed more—namely, skiing.

The time then came for PCS and I wanted to downsize, so what did I do? I posted the jeep on Craigslist, with no responses. Finally, after a month or so, a guy offered me a kit car for it. Wanting something new, and realizing that having an off-road vehicle just wasn't me, I reluctantly traded it. The kit car I received was a 1929 Gazelle replica. (Think Roaring Twenties *Great Gatsby*.) I say reluctantly because I was trying to downsize, not acquire another vehicle. However, the silver lining was that it was drivable across the country. The Jeep was not.

Two duty stations later I finally found time to start restoring my latest purchase. The body was fiberglass and had never been painted before. I had previously painted the Jeep with help from one of the helicopter-maintenance guys at Minot. Among my many projects, I had painted a tractor, my Chevy Suburban, a 1992 Chevy Cavalier (that's another story), and my Kawasaki Ninja.

On all those projects I was always hesitant to clear coat the paint. Clear coating is very difficult if you don't have a lot of experience. If you don't lay it on thick enough, you will get what is known as orange peel, but if

you lay it on too thick, you will get drips, which look horrible, especially with a beautiful glistening paint job.

There I stood with the paint gun in my hand in my makeshift garage paint booth. After countless hours of prepping, sanding, and painting the Gazelle, I began the clear coat. Sure enough, because of all of the curves and unique contours of the car I had built up too heavy of a clear coat in multiple spots while other spots resembled orange peel.

On all my previous restoration jobs I had a few drips, but most were in spots you normally wouldn't see, so I had never attempted to touch them up. These were sticking out like the proverbial sore thumb. I was going to have to do something about them, so it was "YouTube University, here I come."

I watched a couple of videos that scared the crap out of me. The most widely accepted technique was to take a razor blade, hold it perpendicular to the surface of the car, and scrape off the excess clear coat. If you're a car lover, look it up; you'll cringe watching it.

So I opened up my toolbox, took out my razor blade, then headed over to the Gazelle. I looked at the razor blade and then at the car with my reflection shining back at me through the beautiful, shiny clear coat. I stood there frozen with fear, going over what I had to do in my head, and this led me to thinking of all the damage I could do to the paint.

Finally, knowing I had to do it, I scraped, very lightly at first, then noticed it was working just like the videos. This wasn't so bad. Scrape, scrape, scrape. I worked the clear coat down until it was nearly the same level as the rest of the surface. It went from a drip to a hazy white square on the body panel. Step one complete; step two, here I come.

Now I know what you're thinking: the worst was behind me. Nope, the next step required sanding the whole surface of the car with sandpaper. This I also hesitated to do. After I decided to just go for it, the whole car looked like it was covered in white powder. Next came more sanding, then more sanding, but just like I had watched in the videos, the car looked a little better each time I sanded it. After three different grits of sandpaper and three different grits of polish, the Gazelle looked amazing! I stood

there in awe. I had been petrified to damage the paint, but sticking to it and diving in had paid off.

Starting had been the hardest part, but once I got going, there was no turning back, and it became easier and easier. Projects and jobs in the Air Force are no different. You will be challenged with what seem like unattainable goals or projects, but with some direction (in this case, YouTube) and that first step, you can accomplish any goal.

Sure, there may be some missteps along the way, but you learn from them. I have since become better at clear coating, in part because I know that if I screw it up, it can be fixed. You can do anything you put the effort into. The only thing stopping you is you.

The next time you're thinking (or worrying) about how to get started, put that aside and just do something. It may be wrong at first, but you will get on the right track. While working on the light bulb, Thomas Edison learned 1,000 ways how not to make a light bulb before getting it right.

On that same note, at my retirement (my fifteen minutes of fame), I had prepared my speech. I had labored over it for many months and had cut it down to one topic from my original three or four points. I knew from being on the other side in the audience that everyone would just be waiting for it to be over and eyeballing the cake, so I made sure to condense it down to one topic in hopes that I wouldn't lose their attention. It went something like this.

Growing up in the 1980s, we had some great corporate marketing wars such as Coke versus Pepsi and GoBots versus Transformers, but my favorite of all was Nike versus Reebok. It seemed like one of those issues where you were on one side or the other and dared not venture to the competition.

Most of us kids would stay loyal to one side, and the great marketing machine had pushed me toward Reebok. The most distinct commercial that completely pushed me to Reebok was the bungee-jumping video and, yes, "the Pump."

If you have a minute, look it up. For those of you wanting to continue reading, I'll describe it. The scene begins with the image of a bridge, a very high arching bridge well above the river below. The screen flashes to a sign "Do not throw material from bridge."

The next camera shot shows two guys standing on the ledge of the bridge. They are both wearing bungee cords strapped to their feet, one wearing Reebok and the other Nike. They look at one another, then the Reebok guy bends over and pumps up his shoes. It then cuts to a slow-motion series of camera shots as the two of them jump off the bridge at the same time.

In the following scene you see the Reebok guy swinging from the end of the bungee, then the Nike shoes swing by empty. I was hooked. I still have never bungee jumped and never plan on it, but the ad proved its point that if I ever did, I'd better be wearing Reebok Pumps. I incessantly asked my parents for Reebok shoes and would stay loyal to the brand for years. I actually still use Reebok hockey skates.

For all the great marketing Reebok got right, there was one area where they could never compete with Nike. And no, it's not Michael Jordan. It's the slogan, and yes, you probably have already said it in your head well before reading it. "Just do it." What an outstanding and powerful statement. Just do it. Think about it. Anything you have done in life I guarantee you have just done it.

It applies to everything, and when it comes to accomplishing your goals in and outside of your job, I urge you to just do it! There will always be a better time, a better way, a better plan, but as I have mentioned multiple times, getting started is the hardest part. In the words of Bilbo Baggins from *The Hobbit* by J. R. R. Tolkien, *"It's a dangerous business, Frodo, going out of your door. You step into the Road, and if you don't keep your feet, there is no knowing where you might be swept off to."*

Whatever you are looking to do, just do it. Maybe it's a task from your supervisor you're hesitating to do, maybe it's buying that house, maybe it's starting a degree program, maybe it's applying for OTS. There are so many missed opportunities, and you never know what door any of

them might have opened. I used to finish all my emails with one of my favorite quotes after my signature block:

"A good plan violently executed now is better than a perfect plan executed next week."
George S. Patton

This still rings true even after the Air Force.

The final piece of the puzzle

People sometimes have trinkets or items that they believe are good luck. Ever since my first flight I had one. You could always find it in my flight suit top-left pocket, then my left-leg pocket when we switched to two-piece flight suits. It was a little black book. (Not that type of black book—get your head out of the gutter.)

It was the New Testament Bible, given to me by my parents with my name embossed in small gold print on the cover.

I attribute my strength, resilience, and perseverance to my faith. I'm not going to preach to you or attempt to convert you to a certain religion. I want you to find your piece of the puzzle. In hard times, having a higher power to believe in outweighs everything else. Prayer has moved me through both good times and bad. I am so thankful for so many things that God has bestowed upon me.

Find what spiritually speaks to you!

G's lessons learned

Throughout my career I have found many things to motivate me. It may be easy to say I want to be "blank" in ten years, but what often happens is you lose sight of that goal and it becomes a forgotten dream. Instead, aim for small short-term goals.

I am continually changing my goals. For example, to stay in shape I don't just say, "I want to be in better shape." I figure out what big event is coming up shortly and set a goal for that event such as being fit for a hockey tournament I'm going to play in a couple months; or looking good in a bathing suit for my upcoming vacation.

These are only a few examples, and you will discover your own. Getting there is never going to be easy. You have to push through the tough times, and having the grit to do so will pay off.

Great reward requires smart, hard work.

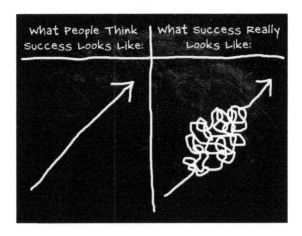

CHAPTER TEN: ADVANCEMENT

Advancement - *the promotion of a person in rank or status.*
["opportunities for career advancement"]

This chapter covers how to better prepare yourself as you climb up the ranks. There are some little-known facts that I didn't learn until I was much older and further into my career that would have helped me at a younger age, and so I'm passing them on to you.

Questions to ask yourself:

- Question 1: How far do you want to go in the Air Force?
- Question 2: Are you prepared to put in some effort to maximize your opportunities?
- Question 3: Do you think timing is everything?

Pay no attention to the man behind the curtain

During the helicopter portion of pilot training, you would be assigned a "stick buddy."

On each flight you would split time with your stick buddy, spending half of the sortie up front actually flying and learning about the aircraft. For the other half, you would sit in the back and provide support by clearing the area for obstacles, birds, and other aircraft. Typically, it wouldn't matter who flew first, but sometimes, especially during check rides, everyone would want to fly first to get it over with.

My stick buddy could speak two languages. He was raised in Korea and was fluent in both English and Korean. Sometimes during the stress of a flight, while sitting in the back, he would be asked a question by the instructor and would hesitate for a bit before responding. Like a cartoon, I pictured the words going into his head, being translated by a little box into Korean, then into another box for English, then out his mouth.

He did very well during training, and I had to give him mad props. Language is not my strong suit, and I couldn't imagine knowing two fluently. After I failed a check ride, we found ourselves on drop night

going to distinctly different locations that would determine our overall career paths.

Off to Minot I went while he went to Andrews AFB near Washington, DC. That's when the biggest change happened. My stick buddy was at a location where there are very highly influential officers in all branches of the military.

During his time there, and doing his job very well, he was selected to be an executive officer for one of the generals. This would catapult his career and allow him to eventually make full bird colonel.

I have sat through many commander mentor sessions, and they typically begin with:

> I'm no different than you were at that point in your career.
> I didn't do anything amazing.
> I was at the right place at the right time.

While all of these points may be true to a certain extent, they always leave out one, and it's probably the most important point: the man behind the curtain.

In most cases, it's a high-ranking officer, but it could also be the right supervisor or a chief. There was always an influential person who guided them through the ranks, and here's a little secret for all you aspiring officers out there: What you do as a captain will determine if you will be a colonel or not. Kind of scary to think, right?!

You are just learning how to be an officer, and people are already planning where you will end up in fifteen years. They are grooming you for that position, and while there are outliers, this is typically the case.

What I suggest to you is to work hard and don't attempt to be a suck-up, but if the opportunity arises and they are looking for the commander's exec, volunteer. Most people hate being an exec because it's all paperwork, but it's also face time with the prime decision-maker. On the enlisted side, volunteer for tough projects and events others are unwilling to take because they might require a lot of work.

One of the reasons I believe I was selected to OTS was my connection to the base commander at Shaw AFB. He was a full bird colonel and would give out a letter of recommendation to whomever he deemed worthy of attending OTS. I had a briefing with him with the crow cart team, and he was present for more than one of my other briefings. My briefings must have made an impression on him and, besides, who can forget a name like Golembiewski!

How to excel and be a good exec—I could write a whole book on the subject, especially with the help of my wife, who has been an exec four times. But I'll keep it simple and just highlight the most important things.

Paper makes the Air Force go 'round. Well, now it's the PDF. As an exec, it is your job to filter all the paperwork that gets funneled to the commander. Ensuring each product is up to speed, with correct spelling, good grammar (except performance reports; more on that later), and signed at the appropriate times will save your commander time and make you a star. With countless meetings, award boards, and other issues that arise on a day-in and day-out basis, time is in short supply.

The second most important task is to ensure awards and performance reports are prepared in a timely fashion and in the way the commander likes it. While the standard layout is always the same for bullets, action, impact, and result, some parts are commander-specific.

For example, I had one commander that only used a colon between the three parts. Yet I had another that only used dashes and another that didn't care as long as all the bullets were the same. I don't want to get into the weeds too much but wanted to highlight some examples.

This can work on the enlisted side as well. Those packages that you will be writing will be sent to a commander eventually. Ask around and save yourself time by setting it up the way the commander likes it. I have seen a performance report go back and forth several times for simple formatting errors. And last, as a junior officer or junior enlisted troop, be prepared to submit the performance report way too early. I'll just leave it at that.

Check the box

You will hear the above term ad nauseum throughout your career. My piece of advice in this area is to do it your way. Just note that if you choose the difficult path, your box will be checked like everyone else's. There is no check plus. Education is amazing and you should never stop learning. Once you settle, turn off learning, and believe you know all you need to know, you have now failed or likely will in the future.

For those of you who I just informed are failures, you don't have to be. Find something you enjoy and learn it your way. It doesn't have to be an accredited school, unless you're going for that piece of paper with your name on it. You can learn so much from local classes, self-help books, that Home Depot guide that details how to tile a bathroom (one of my least favorite activities), and so forth.

After settling into the unit at Fairchild, I thought I had my life in order. Just so you know, life is never in order. I live in chaos, so if you do too, welcome to the club. I decided that the next box to check was a master's degree. I had paid the fee to get a B for my bachelor's degree and decided this one was for me.

If you recall, I had dropped out of college once already, and that was a graphic design program I had attempted. One of my dreams as a kid was to be a Disney animator, and I had actually done a few Claymations and short cartoons during high school. The college thing didn't work out because, well, girls, in particular my then girlfriend. I had chosen graphic design because I thought it was a close second to animation, and the school was close enough to home so I could visit my girlfriend frequently.

Now here I was choosing a very similar major for my master's degree, graphic design. I was excited. This was my choice, and I had been accepted to a prestigious California art school. The classes would all be online, which was one of the motivating factors to not pursuing animation, and tuition assistance from the military was going to pay for it. Well, most of it. Turns out college books are expensive, especially in the arts.

I had used the "Top-Up" program during my bachelor's degree in order to pay nothing out of pocket. Top-Up would cover the amount over what

tuition assistance covered, taking it from your MGIB. So, there I was, navigating the confusing college applications, signing up for the right classes, and moving on to learn some cool stuff. Or so I thought.

My classes began with working through some of the basic courses, such as the history of graphic design, which emphasized both typefaces and fonts. (Yes, they are technically different.) Then it was on to the good stuff of actually designing products, articles, and other fun projects.

I quickly became frustrated, however, not because it was difficult but rather the opposite. I would submit work, being as creative as I could, then be hit with low grades and lots of comments on my mistakes. Turns out I was back in a game. Even in class it was a rigid structure, and I was simply told to regurgitate the assignments verbatim.

In my first semester, I had just learned about all these famous designers who broke the mold and did amazing things. I was then instructed to color in the lines and learn the rules before I could break them. This was a *master's* course, not a bachelor's course. Shouldn't you have to learn the basics in bachelor's courses, then break the rules and venture out into the unknown in master's-level classes? I was sorely mistaken, and this was when I had an epiphany. School was a money grab. They had simplified the course so high schoolers could pass it by simply following the rules.

This turned me into a disgruntled college hater, which was thankfully a short phase. Eventually, I came to realize college has its place, but the frustration I experienced set me on a different career path. More on that later. This may sound like I hate learning, and that is far from the truth. I love learning. I just don't want to spend my hard-earned money on it.

In your Air Force journey, you will be constantly bombarded with advice to continue your education, and I completely support that, but as the saying goes, work smarter, not harder. Today there are countless colleges and universities online. Find the easiest one that will be fully covered by TA, and check the box. If you decide to leave the Air Force and pursue more education, good on you; save your MGIB for that.

Working full time and going to night school takes a toll on you. You

shouldn't put that added stress on yourself, especially when as far as the Air Force is concerned, no one will know where your degree is from. On all packages it will simply state whether you have a degree or not. If it's from Mickey Mouse University or took you five hours a week to accomplish it, as long as it's an accredited school, your package will look exactly the same as someone who earned their degree at Harvard.

Keep all your doors open for as long as possible. Start now if you haven't already. I have heard plenty of people state that they were taking some time off from school, never to get started again. Once you have momentum, use it. It's not just a physics thing. Your mind and routines will already be geared to school, and in the end, the learning will come faster and easier to you.

It's like driving a car. You spend the most energy and fuel to get it moving, then once it's in cruise, the fuel usage goes down. It's the same with school. Check all the boxes, including higher education and Air Force programs. For the officers, that's SOS, Air Staff, and Command College. For enlisted, that's your CDCs and the Community College of the Air Force.

Also find out what is weighted more as a delineator. For example, when I was a captain, the school you would attend was SOS. Maxwell AFB was not able to support the large number of captains at the time, so they had an online course to delineate who was selected to attend. I finished the online course as quickly as possible so I could attend the actual school, but another captain was selected ahead of me even though he didn't finish the online course. I found out after the fact that he had finished his master's degree and that counted more than finishing the online course. These things are always changing, so make sure you get your facts when presented with two or more options.

On that note, a master's degree was used as a qualifier on promotion boards in some years but not in other years. This change occurred at least three different times during my officer career. What do I mean by that? When the board reviews a promotion package, most notably to major and lieutenant colonel, they use a master's degree to sort the candidates into the categories of promote, maybe promote, and don't promote.

There were some years where the master's degree was shown on the package while in others it was not. Err on the side of caution, and just get it done. I know a handful of officers who were not promoted for the simple fact that they didn't have their master's degree, and they were dumbfounded as to why they didn't get promoted.

Remember, be Santa.

Hey, airman, I got another task for you

There is an unwritten rule called the 80/20 rule. It states that you get 80 percent productivity from 20 percent of your effort. This is truly evident in people also, and I saw it every year of my Air Force career.

Where do you want to be? Do you want to just get by and be the 80 percent that holds everyone back or the 20 percent that elevates everyone and helps the unit excel? I hope you said the latter, and if you did, you will feel frustrated.

I've been part of this on the enlisted side, on the officer side, and as a commander delegating tasks. It happens quite often, and if you find a solution send, me a note. If you recall my story of troubleshooting ECM pods, after finding the wire issue, I was chosen to be part of a special electronics team. It was called the crow cart, and the history behind it is very interesting.

The career field of electronic warfare goes back to Vietnam and the mighty F-4, which was used extensively during the Vietnam conflict. One of their missions was destruction of the Soviet surface-to-air missile sites or SAMS. The F-4s used for this mission were labeled Wild Weasels. They would use ECM pods to jam enemy radar and remain undetected during the attack run.

Technology was very primitive and there were a lot of issues, but that was the birth of the ECM pod, and along with it came the Radar Warning Receiver or RWR system. This system would detect an enemy SAM and would display it to the aircrew on a round screen. The symbols that appeared on-screen would depict a SAM's location and what frequency was being used to "paint" the aircraft. The aircrew would then tell the ECM pod what frequency to jam.

Fast-forward to the year 2000 at Shaw AFB, South Carolina. I had been chosen to be part of the crow cart team, and the system we were testing was the RWR of the F-16. The crow cart was the brainchild of our civilian ECM technician. He had an extensive knowledge of electronics and was our go-to guy when we couldn't figure out a fault. He was also one of my mentors who nudged me to get away from just pulling cards. Now, after being selected to the crow cart, we found that of the entire F-16 fleet, only 20 percent of the RWR systems were working properly.

I often wondered if they told the pilots about the failures or if the commander kept it to himself. Needless to say, this issue was highlighted, and we even went to Hill AFB, Utah, to test their F-16s. During this testing phase, I was also selected to be the official briefer for the dog and pony show we held to explain what the crow cart did.

I would be fixing aircraft one day, practicing a briefing the next, followed by briefing a full bird colonel or general the day after that. Then after all the demonstrations, there was an aircraft accident. No, it wasn't with the RWR; it was a brake failure. However, there was a special tasking about it that I was selected for, so my superiors added more to my extra duties.

While flying around Charleston AFB, South Carolina, an F-16 pilot realized he had a brake issue. After burning off fuel, he decided to land and utilize the arresting cable, which is typically seen and used extensively on aircraft carriers, but for this situation the airfield would raise the cable from the ground.

The aircraft has a hook hanging from its belly, and as it rolled over the cable, the hook would snatch it and the bungee-like strap would stop the aircraft almost instantaneously. In this instance, the cable was either not attached or failed on one side. This caused the aircraft to whiplash off the runway, hitting a concrete barrier, shearing off the nose gear.

So how did this all affect me?

The F-16 had one of our ECM pods on the belly, which was also sheared in half horizontally. In an effort to save money, our shop was tasked with taking that damaged pod and another ECM pod from a previous accident and making one good pod. Who did they choose to be part of the team?

You guessed it: this guy. Then shortly after finishing the project, China intervened.

Back in 2000 at Shaw AFB we were known to have "short" pods, while Hill AFB had "long" pods. What's the difference? Why, the length, of course. In addition to that, the short pod was all digital whereas the long pod had an additional section that housed analog components.

The threats of the day all used digital frequencies, but guess what? China pulled out all their ancient Soviet technology. To counter this, I was then put on a team to take our long sections from the boneyard and integrate them with our short pods.

Shortly after beginning this project, I was selected for Officer Training School. It seemed the more I would do, and do well, the more I was tasked with. This happens every day all over the world, not just in the Air Force.

As my career progressed, I found myself as a flight commander, and this enabled me to see the other side of the equation. I would be tasked with choosing someone to accomplish something. It never mattered who I chose, since if they couldn't handle the project or task, it would inevitably end up with the person with the most additional duties. It would always get accomplished because that individual almost always was accomplishing more than their peers.

If you're reading this, I'm guessing you are or will be part of the hard-working 20 percent, and I don't want you to ever get discouraged. The effort will lead to better and better things. There is a path out there for you. Stay the course, and in the end, you will look back at it and say, "Wow, I did all that."

As I'm writing this, I keep remembering opportunities and events I was able to participate in and how all the effort has been worth it. People miss opportunities all the time; don't fall into that trap.

Seize the day!

And the award goes to. . .

I finished my workout, hit the showers, then proceeded into the office. After sitting down to check my email, I noticed there was a message reminding us of an awards board later that afternoon. I continued my work for the day, and as the meeting rolled around, I headed to our briefing room.

There all the flight commanders sat around a large table. Having no assigned seating, I took the first open chair. We all waited patiently as a few stragglers came in, then someone called the room to attention when the squadron commander entered. After we were put at ease, the meeting began.

The executive officer pulled up some slides with "Quarterly Awards" written at the top. Below the header sat multiple categories such as "Airman of the Month" and "Instructor of the Quarter". The executive officer would start at the top, stating, "Airman of the Quarter: who are your candidates?" We would go around the room submitting the individual we believed was worthy of that award and then debate who should win at the squadron level in order to submit a package to the group level.

Typically, there would be one person who clearly deserved the award, but there were other times when the determining factor would be who won last quarter. You guessed it. To a small extent, the "play the game and get a trophy" mindset had infiltrated the military. I bring this up for two reasons.

First, as you work hard to prove yourself, don't get discouraged if you don't win all the awards. There will be times when you think you were overlooked but, in reality, you were neck and neck with someone else, and it wasn't your turn.

Continue to work hard, and more often than not, you will be rewarded for your efforts. At the end of the day, they know who the hard workers and motivated individuals are. The commander knows, regardless of how many awards you win, who they will be sending down the fast track.

Second, as you climb the ranks and are in the position to select winners and provide your feedback, remember how it would feel if you worked your tail off then lost out because you had your turn last quarter. There are always going to be things beyond our control, including biases, whether we admit them or not, but don't let that keep you down or demotivate you.

When time comes for you to make the decision, remember how you would want it to be on the receiving end. I would never personally want to win unless I earned it. The universe has a way of making things work out, and if you put in your time and effort, you WILL reap the rewards.

On the topic of awards, don't be a ribbon seeker. I've seen this on both the enlisted and officer side. What do I mean by that? While I was at Andrews AFB, we received the first two upgraded aircraft with a new avionics package. The commander was selecting what we called the initial cadre.

What initial cadre entailed was learning the system, device, or weapon from an outside source, such as civilians or another military organization, and then training the unit's instructors. This would then turn into a normal training event where the instructors would continue to train the unit.

I was approached by the commander to be part of the initial cadre. By this point in my career, I had set my path in stone. I had intentionally not accomplished my master's, for reasons I have previously described, and never finished the ACSC online course. I enjoyed flying and wanted to stay at the squadron level.

Due to my prior enlisted time, I didn't have to worry about the potential of separating due to not making rank. I knew my path and understood that being part of the initial cadre, while I would be good at it, should be left for a younger and just as capable instructor. While issues arose and, eventually, I reluctantly took on the task, I wasn't chasing awards and I knew that it would be an exceptional bullet for an OPR or awards package.

On the flip side, I have seen multiple times where "good deals" and great opportunities for a more than capable airman arose only to have a

senior individual take the task, just because it was a cool thing and they knew they could do it. If you are ever in the position to help support the maturation and growth of a junior member by turning down a "good deal," do it.

As a young copilot at Minot, I got to see an example of this from the good side. After one of our helicopters reached a certain number of hours, it would be flown to Cherry Point in North Carolina for an overhaul. They would disassemble the entire aircraft and inspect the parts for fatigue cracks, corrosion, and any other mechanical defects. This would happen typically once a year for only one of our six aircraft, and some years we didn't have a Cherry Point run.

In those days there was very little in "off-station" training that allowed us to fly outside of the local area. Occasionally we would fly down to Bismarck, get lunch, then fly home, and this was a big deal at the time.

Being selected to fly to Cherry Point was a high honor as not everyone got to do it, and the experience of flying halfway across the country was invaluable. On one trip, we had to circumnavigate the weather, landing at airports we had never been to and navigating states I had never seen from the air. It was such an amazing way to learn.

This all could have been taken by someone senior to me.

Did you see the game last night? It was incredible.

It was 6:00 p.m. on a Tuesday night. I deboarded the helicopter, collected my flight gear, turned the aircraft over to maintenance, then headed into the squadron.

I checked in my helmet to get it cleaned, hung up my armored vest and survival gear, and headed to my office to do one last check of the email before heading home. I made my way up the stairs past the now dark ops desk. We were the last flight of the day, and the team manning the desk had closed up as soon as we had shut down our engines.

As I continued down the hall to my office, I noticed another office light on, so I headed over to see who was still there. It was one of our schedulers.

"How's it going?" I asked. "You're here pretty late."

"I have so much work to do and I need to get it done," the scheduler responded with a much-stressed tone in his voice.

"That sucks," I said, then headed to my office to accomplish what I had set to do.

Upon finishing my task, I popped in to say bye to the scheduler, then headed home. This would happen a lot in the unit with different individuals. You might be thinking, *I totally get it; there is so much work to do and not enough time!*

I'm sure the majority of people would agree with you, but I disagree. You see, our scheduler had spent nearly all morning at the ops desk talking with people, wandering around the squadron, accomplishing a task here or there, but mostly talking. Time management.

Next time you say you don't have time to accomplish your job, retrace your steps. Were you talking about last night's Final Four game for hours? Maybe it was your fantasy football team or that amazing movie that just came out. Humans are social creatures—I get that. I play fantasy football, and as a matter of fact, it was around that time when I started.

You have to manage your time, which may mean you debate who should be drafted first in your fantasy football league for twenty minutes instead of forty. The more tasks I was given throughout my career, the more I tried to figure out the quickest and most efficient ways to get them done. I've seen some people reinstall doors that had been previously removed to allow for some dedicated time behind a closed door to accomplish a set of tasks.

Most people are procrastinators. If you wait until the last minute, it only takes you a minute, right? This has an effect that can not only hurt you but also the unit. Take a performance report, for example. It is due on a specific date, and then there is the month later when it's actually due. Depending on how far from the top that individual is, I've seen deadlines pushed out from the scheduled due date, sometimes up to two months.

Could you imagine taking a class for two months and the teacher tells you the final exam is two weeks *before* your last class?

All this because we are all procrastinators, and leadership attempts to "help" the situation by adding more "time" to finish the report. What happens is that a couple of days before the report's new due date is when it actually gets looked at or finished.

Personally, I would rather front-load my pain by getting the work done right away and then sit back and relax. This sometimes became very difficult because if I finished earlier, I was hurting my rate. As a supervisor, I often needed to allow folks the whole period to complete and excel in a task so that I could add it to their performance reports.

There are also times when you will be awaiting someone else to finish a task that involves you but that you have no control over. For three years straight I had to come in on leave to sign my OPR because people procrastinated.

I digress. Look at your surroundings and figure out ways to be productive. If you have a quiet place to work with a door, close it and give yourself enough time to accomplish your tasks.

Trust me, getting your work done without staying late is well worth it and overall is more important than harassing the guy you just stomped in fantasy football.

Screen time need not apply

"Hey, I have this great program to stream music on your computer; you should install it," I heard a character say on my computer screen. The nicely dressed gentleman was hovering over my cubicle in the online game. I had two choices. Accept and install the program or turn him down. I clicked on the "turn him down" button and heard my character respond, "No thanks."

This will be the joy you will face every year: annual Computer-Based Training (CBTs). You will have to complete multiple training

modules each year, some over the course of the year. This can be frustrating, but I would set aside a day or two to accomplish it all.

Remember, I like to front-load the pain. Give yourself about a week's buffer. There has been a time or two where I wasn't on top of my deadlines and let a certificate expire only to spend extra time getting it fixed.

In today's workplace, not only in the Air Force, countless hours are spent on the computer. This includes computer-based training, and much of that training has to do with protocols for logging in and sending or receiving emails. There are a lot of people out there trying to do some pretty bad things with spyware and such, so you need to know the correct procedures to follow to mitigate the threats.

It's kind of humorous that we restrict screen time from our children, but we ourselves spend the majority of the day staring at a computer screen. Now, not every job is this way. When I was in maintenance, I was on my feet repairing the equipment, mopping floors, and doing other labor tasks, but we still had email.

As you progress in your career, you will find yourself with more and more screen time. Performance reports need to be written, awards packages put together, and a response sent to the email that your PT test is next week.

There is some truth to the "Chair Force" jokes that go around but just remember, they're jealous. For those of you with mainly sedentary jobs plugging numbers and working with the computer, remember to take care of yourself. Get up and walk around. As supervisors, remember to work with the younger troops because this is where you can be a leader instead of a boss.

Don't get overwhelmed with all the additional duties, as there will be many. The latest trend is desks that convert to standing desks. If you don't have one, ask, and I'm sure with the end-of-year funds you can get one. Some of this goes back to your personal fitness. Get up, move, stretch, and take frequent breaks. Wow, I feel like I'm warning you before playing Nintendo Wii. Move that lamp out of the way while you're at it.

Another issue facing us today is cell phones. Everyone has one, and everyone is always using them. In my last few years, people would be continually on their phones, sometimes when they should have been working. Overall, during ceremonies, briefings, and other formal events, phones were put away and everyone acted professionally, i.e., as adults.

When you're communicating with someone face-to-face, put the phone away. I would occasionally take notes with an app on my phone, but I would tell the person I was talking to exactly what I was doing. I still felt a little awkward, but I wanted to make sure I had the information right. Technology is great but know when to put it away.

The myth of boss vs. leader

One day I was standing at our operations desk planning for a sortie. During discussion, I had mentioned that a good commander would give a task and then turn to other issues. I was met with some fierce opposition. "That's a boss, not a leader" was the retort.

Recently there have been plenty of memes on social media about a boss versus a leader. The one that comes to mind is a depiction of three men pulling a stone with ropes while another man sits on top of the boulder and points to where they need to go. In that picture is the word "Boss."

Below this is a picture of the same three men dragging the same stone, but in this depiction the fourth man is pulling alongside the first three men. The text in this picture reads "Leader."

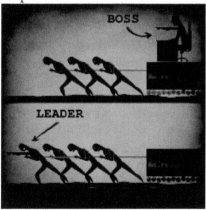

Yep, that's the one!

While I understand the general meaning, I believe the message is a little off. In my opinion, the fourth man shouldn't even be in the picture. Now hear me out. There are situations where this graphic depiction may be true, but in the Air Force that is hardly the case.

The Air Force is built on structure. Each member has their role to play, just like a sports team. Take the great game of football. In this example, let's look at the defensive team. Their objective is to stop the offense from advancing the ball. To do so, each member has their job to do.

If the linebacker tries to help out a lineman, he vacates the position he was supposed to be in, creating a gap, weakening the defense, and eventually allowing the offense to exploit that weakness. My comment about the commanders has to do with empowering their people and moving on to tasks that only commanders can complete.

It is like this at every level. During our ramp-up at F. E. Warren, we had been authorized to fly with M240 machine guns. In order for us to fly with them and be able to utilize them if a threat arose, we had to train.

Prior to our training sorties, the ammunition would have to be broken out of the storage boxes, assembled, then mounted in cans that attach to the weapon during training. This was the job of the flight engineers because the pilots had to plan the flight, prepare the aircraft, and coordinate the range times.

If I as an aircraft commander were down in the weeds loading ammo cans, the planning would never get done, or essentially the commander would be doing two tasks. As I have seen both sides of the equation, starting off as enlisted then moving to the office world, I know everyone has a specific job to do.

Leaders have a lot going on behind the scenes. Just because you don't always see it, don't think they are just being a boss when in reality they are working hard to be a good leader.

G's lessons learned

If you are aspiring to climb the ranks and (let's be honest, who isn't), don't step on your friends to climb to victory. Life is a team sport.

If you want to make it, then you have to play the game and check the boxes, and you'll have the extra credit of a friend in your corner of the boxing ring to propel you on.

Find your Mickey (not the mouse, Mick from *Rocky*), take that mentor's advice, and run with it.

CHAPTER ELEVEN: NATION

Nation - a large body of people united by common descent, history, culture, or language, inhabiting a particular country or territory.
["the world's leading industrialized nations"]

This chapter covers your "AF Nation" and how becoming closer to your unit will make life more fun and enjoyable. You will have opportunities to help out others and in doing so it will benefit you as well.

Questions to ask yourself:

- Question 1: How well do you play with others?
- Question 2: Are you an organizer? Could you become one?
- Question 3: If you are an introvert, do you see the importance of belonging and being part of a team?

All for one

I arrived at the unit around 2100 local time. There at the ops desk stood my director of operations (DO) and one of our flight engineers. "Your copilot is pre-flighting the aircraft," the DO stated as I walked through the door. I watched the flight engineer rush past me and out the door.

Suddenly the duty desk officer shot up from his chair. "Here are the coordinates," he stated as he slid a yellow sticky note over toward me on the desktop. "JRCC has approved the launch."

I gathered myself and headed to the planning room. On the way, I grabbed the topographical maps required for the search area. I had been on many search and rescue missions, but this one started off differently. Most scenarios began with someone hiking and then getting lost or injuring themselves, but not this one.

Typically, the ones we were searching for were ordinary people, most likely with little experience in the outdoors, but the missing person in this case was a search and rescue volunteer. I was reminded of the scene in *Saving Private Ryan* when the medic wants to join the fight. "Who's going to fix you if you get hit?" a soldier asked him. This seemed

like that. The person who was supposed to be doing the saving needed saving.

 It was a Saturday night, my copilot was at the aircraft, and based on previous launches, so was my flight engineer, who ran out as soon as I arrived. In the planning room, I prepared my flight map, adding waypoints into the system, figuring out how long it would take to get there, determining our loiter time over the search area, and locating the nearest refueling points and local hospital pads in the event we needed to deliver the patient to one.

I finished up and received a few more details about the ground party— namely, the radio frequency and contact call sign of the search and rescue team. I gathered my helmet, survival bag, and flight gear, then headed out to the hangar.

I arrived to find the aircraft outside, my copilot sitting in his seat, and the flight engineer testing the rescue hoist by dragging the cable up and down into a large bucket. As soon as I climbed into the aircraft and donned my helmet, the copilot hit the starter. Within minutes we were airborne and heading east to Silver Mountain.

While in route to Silver Mountain, I gathered the map and my kneeboard, which had the survivor's last known location along with other details. I input the coordinates into the GPS, and my copilot slightly changed course to ensure we were headed in the right direction. I briefed the crew on everything I knew and in turn was filled in with some additional facts.

In no time, we were approaching the mountain. Earlier that day on Silver Mountain ski resort, volunteers were flagging and setting up a mountain bike course for a race they were going to host. The volunteers had ATVs and were riding the whole day, placing flags at all the turn points so the riders would know where to go.

That afternoon the team gathered to find out how the work was going, but one individual was missing. They began a search, but as the afternoon turned to evening, they knew they needed help. That was when we were requested for support.

142

One guy on an ATV somewhere on the north face of Silver Mountain. Got it.

Upon arriving, we established radio communications with the course volunteers who were now the ground search team. We began our passes, searching in a zigzag pattern starting at the top of the mountain and working our way down. We briefed each other on search boundaries, which were the locations we would not extend past on each leg of our search.

If you haven't been to Silver Mountain, there are places where the trees are dense. Our search area consisted almost entirely of pine trees averaging about fifty feet tall. This meant we almost had to look straight down into the foliage if we were to have any hopes of finding someone.

A few passes into our search, our flight engineer decided he would attempt to use our FLIR (Forward-Looking Infrared Ball). Now this thing was ancient. I think it was designed in the '60s, and it was horrible. I know some of you are probably thinking of the movie *Predator* with thermal imaging. Nope, think Atari graphics looking at trees all in green.

Our flight engineer began swinging the FLIR around, doing his best. Between me and my copilot, we attempted to fly as smoothly as possible since any large turns or aggressive maneuvers would disrupt the image.

After some time, we heard, "I'm taking a break," from the back of the aircraft, shortly followed by the sound of puking. Our crusty old previous MH-53 special operations flight engineer was hanging out the side of the helicopter throwing up all over the place. It was at this point we began to roll out of our turn to fly straight and level to help reduce his feelings of sickness. We were greeted with, "No, continue turn; I think I saw something."

My copilot marked the map for a potential sighting, and I continued the turn. "I see some reflectors—there's the ATV," we heard from the back. We continued to orbit and noticed the ATV was flipped over and nobody was around. We began to expand our search out from where the ATV was spotted.

143

Shortly after expanding the search, we spotted somebody walking alone down a dirt road, and we came to a hover over him. He looked up and then began walking again like a zombie, like he had no idea where he was or what he was doing. We radioed the ground team, who mounted their ATVs and began driving down the mountain. We could see all the ATV lights snaking from one side of the mountain to the other as they used the switchbacks to make their way down.

We began to orbit the area as we waited for the ground team to arrive. Shortly after the ground team met up with the survivor, it was determined he was in pretty bad shape. We were asked to find a location to land and quickly found a suitable spot in a small field near a parking lot at the base of the mountain. Once we landed, we were met by the ground team who loaded the survivor, and we headed off to the nearest hospital. We successfully dropped off the survivor and proceeded home.

Being in the Air Force is a team sport. There are days when you get to do missions such as that night on Silver Mountain, but most of the time, it's gathering data and doing the daily grind. At the end of the day everyone is needed, important, and invaluable to the execution of the overall mission.

There are days when you will feel what you're doing isn't making a difference, but it is. You hear about missions like Silver Mountain and may feel your job isn't as valuable. However, everyone is extremely important to every mission. Everything you do is something someone else doesn't have to do or, even more importantly, can't do.

When I first entered the Air Force and was working maintenance, there were plenty of days of mind-numbing troubleshooting. We didn't have much going on. All the aircraft were in the States accomplishing training. It was repetitive work, and it seemed every time we were on schedule, a crew chief would show up with a "cold-soaked" pod to liven things up.

As F-16 pilots run their checklists, there are certain sequences they follow, one being to turn on their Electronic Countermeasures (ECM) pod. If they missed this step on the ground and proceeded to turn it on at altitude, the intense heat the pod generated would cause condensation on the electronic equipment inside the pod. If there was enough moisture, some of the circuit boards would short-circuit.

Upon return of the flight, the pod would be offloaded and sent to us. We would then have to perform tests to ensure all the systems were working properly. Inevitably something would be malfunctioning, and we would start the task of troubleshooting. This could end up taking days, sometimes weeks, if it was really having issues. It was during these times I saw some good and some bad teamwork.

As happens in a lot of shops and jobs, we would get in a competition. Day shift versus night shift. It was a race to see who could fix it faster, and this brought each shift together. The longer a pod was taking to fix, the more everyone gave their input, some good and some bad. Wading through it all was sometimes a challenge. I always felt defeated when I would come in the next morning to find the pod gone, but that was good because it meant the team won, that pod was fixed, and we could go on to the next one.

The Air Force loves to teach all the academics before moving into actually touching the planes. So, after finishing the academic portion of our pilot training, we finally hit the flight line. This was around the time *Harry Potter* hit the theaters back in 2001. My wife had asked me if I wanted to go see the premier and, not thinking, I said sure. I was unaware it was the midnight showing the night before I was supposed to hit the flight line.

Sounds like a recipe for success, right? That morning, well, let's just say I got a good night's sleep. I woke up frantic when I saw the time. I rushed into the classroom around lunchtime. I had missed morning stand up! This was held every day, and on the first day they would do a demonstration.

The instructor in charge each day would pick a student. Next, the instructor stood behind a briefing stand while the student stood at the other end of the room across one of the longest tables I'd ever seen (think *Batman*, the Michael Keaton one).

The instructor then presented a scenario and asked the student what they would do. You worked through the problem hoping to never hear the words "sit down," which meant you failed. I had missed the whole demonstration, and on top of that, the instructors had to know I was missing.

When I arrived in the classroom, my fellow students were there alone. The instructor hadn't arrived yet. After explaining what had happened and getting a bunch of laughs, they informed me that they covered for me, but I was now the class *Snack-o*. More on that later.

If you have ever watched a good sports movie, the group becomes closer and perseveres as a team no matter how difficult the struggles are. In my experience, the more stressful an environment is, the stronger and closer the team will become.

"It was the best of times; it was the worst of times"

I had just graduated from aircraft commander upgrade. It had been a long journey, and I was finally going to get the keys to the car. I would soon be flying with copilots and would make the final decision on what to do. I was riding high, even though I was heading back to Minot. I arrived in town and headed home.

The following day was Sunday and, as the procedure called for in the day, I called one of the unit pilots. He had been my sponsor when I arrived over a year ago, and while I got situated, he let me stay at his house.

As he answered the phone, he didn't sound quite right. Not thinking much of it, I asked him what time I had to be in the following morning. I was excited to get back to work and start flying again, as I knew I would have to have a couple of flights in the unit before they would officially make me an aircraft commander. Only a few more days of Copilot G.

"Six a.m. in blues," I heard the voice say on the other end of the line.

I hesitated "No, for real. What time do I need to be in?"

"Six a.m. Call anybody else, they'll tell you the same."

"Why?" I asked.

"I can't talk about it," was the response.

I thought about it for a minute then replied, "Okay," and hung up the phone.

I started thinking about what it could be. Had I done something? Then I thought maybe it was a prank. I had fallen for a good one when I was enlisted. I was given a note saying Captain Dee called, and I needed to call and talk to him. Being young, naive, and from Michigan (I'll explain in a minute), I called the number.

"Hello?" the operator answered.

"Yes, is Captain Dee available? I was given a note to call him." There was a pause on the line.

"I'm sorry. I think someone has played a prank on you."

I thanked her and hung up the phone. I had called a local chain fast-food restaurant, "Captain Dee's." I had no clue! Growing up in Michigan, we had Long John Silver's and Colonel Sanders, but I had never heard of Captain Dee's.

So there I was in a similar situation, and something didn't seem right. I decided to take the gamble and gathered together my dress blues uniform. I hadn't worn it since my graduation from pilot training, so it took me a bit to track down all the pieces, but I finally found everything.

The next morning, I woke up early to make sure I could get to work well before 0600. I pulled into the parking lot and made my way upstairs. I found a few people already there in our large briefing room, and they were in dress blues. No, I hadn't been *Punk'd*!

That joy turned quickly into fear when I saw how everyone else looked. "What's going on?" I asked one of my fellow pilots.

"Can't talk about it," he responded.

I asked another with the same answer. Then another. After the third I just stopped and stood in silence.

Just prior to 0600, one of our senior pilots had us form a half circle facing the two entrances to the room. Shortly after we were in

position, the room was called to attention. The wing commander entered in a fury, screaming at the top of his lungs.

Visions of basic training flashed in my head, and much like there, I had no idea why this little ball of rage was yelling at us. The only phrase I remember understanding was that we let down one of our own. The commander left as quickly as he had appeared, our squadron commander then put us at ease, and the new rules were laid out.

The dark ages were about to begin.

Through some investigation, I was able to find out most of the story. My selling point was that I was being punished so I'd at least like to know what happened.

It turns out one of our pilots had his going away party with a lot of alcohol involved. After the party, one of our enlisted troops was too intoxicated to drive, so the owner of the house, also one of our pilots, offered to let him stay the night in the spare bedroom.

This all sounds good, right? Looking out for your team. What happened next is up for debate. The pilot caught the enlisted troop with his girlfriend, and she said she was being raped. As a result, it was mandated that all military protocol would be strictly followed. No personal effects on our desks. No more parties or hanging out and absolutely no alcohol.

This really killed my promotion party a few months later, as it was tradition to buy beer for the unit and throw a party. I remember it was like a funeral. Not fun at all.

It was during this time that my wife headed off to California for "medical school," but I already knew what was going on and flying became a chore.

The restrictions went on for months, but slowly some of them were lifted. We had some new copilots arrive, and suddenly I was becoming one of the old guys. I went back to Kirtland for my instructor upgrade, and when I returned, the unit was changing. All the old guard was almost gone, and most of the new regime hadn't been around for that dark day. The renaissance had arrived!

148

I began really stepping up my workout routine. The unit started hanging out, not only during the week, but we would also take weekend trips up to Lake Metigoshe in the Turtle Mountains. I would bring my boat, and we would waterski, wakeboard, and tube. The guys would bet on how fast I could dump a tuber, and I think that's where I saw the highest vertical ascent of a tube in my life. It was so high the rider had time to jump off at the peak and do a perfect dive into the lake.

We would camp out together, have cookouts, hit up movies, and the camaraderie grew continually. All this filtered over to the day-to-day, and work became fun. Flights were no longer a chore, and I was back to enjoying flying.

Camaraderie is infectious. Make the most out of these situations, as they won't be there forever. If your unit doesn't have a planner, become the planner. Don't force it, but nurture it and let it grow on its own.

Prior to the renaissance, I mainly kept to myself, but after we got some new faces (and I got over my negative feelings), I became a planner. Now, I can't take all the credit. The true planner was my current wife, who had just arrived in the unit as I came back from instructor school. She taught me how to get people together and build camaraderie through fun events.

Later we would start to hold murder mystery dinners, and we still do it to this day. Some of the best units I was a part of were in locations with little to do, so the unit would become closer and do activities together. With social media, people can get sucked into their own little world and never come out. They live on their phones, through their friends, and with people they have never met who live halfway across the country.

Hang out with your unit, even if you only find one other like-minded individual. Instead of envying those people on Facebook with their perfect lives, become them. Bring people along, and share the fun! Units are typically big enough and have quite a wide range of personalities, so you will surely find people you enjoy being around. As an introvert myself, I find when I make the effort to coordinate parties or lunches, I have a good time. You should try it too.

Always find people to enjoy your time with because you may not always have it. I know people who have left the military and have straight up said, "I don't know how to make friends." Once they separated from the military, they became members of a very corporate lifestyle where the clock hits quitting time and everyone scatters to the wind.

Having the same employer right now (the US Government) already gives you something in common; the next step is to dig deeper. Some of the bonds you make in the Air Force will last a lifetime. My best friend I met during my times at Minot, and we continue to keep in touch and use each other for support.

Enjoy your Air Force time. You will have great stories for the rest of your life.

Basic Training April 1999

We all start somewhere. Where you end up is up to you!

G's lessons learned

Feeling wanted and surrounded by friends and people who have something in common always propels a group to greatness.

Ever heard a story, watched a movie, or been part of a group that is going through tough times? I have, and what typically happens is one of two things: they crumble and fail, or more often than not they get stronger like metal folded on metal.

They grow through adversity, and the closer they are, the more resilient they become. If you haven't figured it out yet, success and winning are fun and having a team to enjoy them with is one of the greatest joys in life.

Grab life by the horns.

CHAPTER TWELVE: FINAL THOUGHTS

First, I hope you enjoyed my book. If there were things I left out or that you would like to learn more about, you can always send me an email.

My main goal was to give you a little knowledge on how to set yourself up for success not only in the Air Force but in life in general. I started as a naive teenager, but I eventually matured and was able to not only thrive as an officer and a pilot but set myself up for success after my Air Force career.

The Air Force along with my family and Christian upbringing made me who I am today. There were many ups and down, throughout my career, but they all shaped me into a thriving adult. I am grateful for all of my experiences and have strived to learn from them and never give up.

My biggest piece of advice is to never give up, never get too low, always take the first step, and give it all you've got. There will be times when fear stops you, especially fear of the unknown, but don't let it. You will never know everything, and you will never be the best the first time you try. It often takes failure to propel us to achieve our goals.

As you look ahead at your future, think of where you want to be. Find somebody who has been there to be a mentor, but know that your path will be your own. You will have some difficulties and failures where you will feel like the effort was worthless, but as they say, water finds its level, and eventually you will get to where you want to go.

The next time you are hit with a last-minute tasking, remember once it's done you will have a break, but then another one will come, so don't get too comfortable. There's something about knowing the struggle will be there that makes it easier to cope with, rather than being surprised by it.

If you want to excel, stand out. To stand out you need to put in the effort. This doesn't mean staying late every day; it means working smarter, minimizing cooler talk, and most importantly, just doing it.

The Air Force will ultimately put you in a position to succeed.
Take it and soar!

Last flight in the mighty "Huey"
Here's wishing you blue skies and safe landings.

CHAPTER THIRTEEN BONUS: PERFORMANCE REPORT WRITING

CliffsNotes on performance reports

Thinking about the awesome work you did

Turning ideas into bullets

Action | Impact | Result

You will hear these terms over and over again. Learning to write performance reports is a skill unto itself, but follow these simple steps and it will help you navigate the very unique product known as the EPR and OPR.

First and foremost, you should never write your own report. You should give the highlights of your accomplishments to your supervisor, and they should do the hard work of crafting your report. If they are any good, they will already know most of the projects you worked on and will more than likely only need details, such as how many ammo cans you moved or people you trained. Now onto my proven techniques.

Step One: Don't reinvent the wheel! There will inevitably be somebody who had the same job and same additional duties. In addition, there will be a section on the report that remains the same for everyone, and you can simply cut and paste it. Find the bullets that apply to you, and add them to your report.

Step Two: If you only found one bullet that applies to you in Step One, don't fret. This part was the hardest for me. I don't know how many hours I wasted staring at the white void of a performance report. All that white space! I felt like I needed ski goggles. So, what to do? Just type! It's that simple, even if your bullet looks like this:

- *Painted the wall, it looked great and the commander loved it*

Score! You have something. Now do that with the next line, then the next.

Step Three: Your report will now have minimal white space. It doesn't matter how bad you think your information is. There is something positive about that white space being gone. Remember, the first run is always the hardest. Now we refine each bullet. For example:

- *Meticulously hand designed wall-eliminated cancer forming mold-Rdcd unit member sickness by 99%*
  or
- *Juggernaut momentum crushing wall: Saved 20 labor hours: reduced disassembly cost by $1.2M*

Step Four: Format the information per your commander's desires, and then make the bullets fit—which is usually the trickiest part. Some units let you get away with your own abbreviations, and some have standard ones you have to use. There are also sometimes words you can't use, so ask around for what these are. Remember, this is a team sport.

Step Five: Submit your report and watch it get completely rewritten. I joke, but this will happen to some extent. The more details you know about your unit's standards for PRs, the easier it will be to get it finalized.

Important Note: After the report is submitted, follow up and make sure you're going to be local around the time the report will go final. As mentioned previously, for three years in a row I had to go in to sign my report while away on leave that I had planned months before.

Remember, nobody cares what you actually type in your first draft. Have fun with it at the start, and the creative juices will start flowing.

ACRONYMS

A1C	Airman First Class (E-3)
AC	Aircraft Commander
ACSC	Air Command and Staff College
ADO	Assistant Director of Operations
AFELA	Air Force Educational Leave of Absence
ASVAB	Armed Services Vocational Aptitude Battery
BAH	Basic Allowance for Housing
BDU	Battle Dress Uniform
CBT	Computer-Based Training
CCAF	Community College of the Air Force
CDC	Career Development Course
CHU	Containerized Housing Unit
COLA	Cost Of Living Allowance
CRM	Crew Resource Management
CRS	Component Repair Squadron
ECM	Electronic Countermeasures
EI	Electrical Information
EPR	Enlisted Performance Report
FBO	Fixed Base Operator
FLIR	Forward-Looking Infrared
IMC	Instrument Meteorological Conditions
JAOIT	Joint Air Operations Advisor Team
JRCC	Joint Rescue Coordination Center
LOC	Letter of Counseling
LZ	Landing Zone
MC	Mechanical Comprehension

MEPS	Military Entrance Processing Station
NVG	Night Vision Goggles
OPR	Officer Performance Report
OTS	Office Training School
PC	Political Correctness
PDF	Portable Document Format
PIC	Pilot in Command
PRK	Photorefractive Keratectomy
PT	Fitness Test
RWR	Radar Warning Receiver
SIC	Second in Command
SOS	Squadron Officer School
SrA	Senior Airman (E-4)
TDY	Temporary Duty Assignment
TI	Technical Instructor
TRF	Tactical Response Force
UPT	Undergraduate Pilot Training

LINKS

airforce.com
afreserve.com
recruiting.af.mil
rosecoloredwater.com/two-years-air-force-changed-life/
airmanvision.com
foreverwingman.com
thebalancecareers.com/enlisting-in-the-air-force-3344537
facebook.com/groups/371975880842665 (basic training)

FACEBOOK GROUPS

facebook.com/groups/foreverwingman
facebook.com/groups/MilitaryHumorAndMore
facebook.com/groups/airforceots

PODCASTS

Basic to Blues
CommissionED: The Air Force Officer Podcast
The Professionals Playbook

ACKNOWLEDGEMENTS

There are so many individuals and organizations that have shaped me into who I have become—too many to name all of them individually. However, there are some who must be acknowledged.

First and foremost, I thank God for giving me the skills, demeanor, personality, and faith to defeat my demons and grow as a Christian, an Air Force officer, a husband, and a father.

Special thanks to my parents for raising me with a blue-collar can-do attitude, teaching me to never give up, and instilling a solid moral compass in me; my wife Jenn, without whose support I could not have made my dreams realities; and my two boys, Tynan and Toran, who keep me on my toes and motivate me to attempt to leave this world better than I found it.

Thanks to my oustanding editor, Lisa Tynan and proofreader Rachael Clements. My book would have been a disaster without your expertise.

Finally, I would like to thank the United States Air Force, including all the men and women I served with, both those I knew and the ones I may never meet; my commanders who put me on the path I followed; and the chiefs who checked me when I was a little out of sorts.

EPILOGUE

"See you tomorrow," I said to my friend as we walked out of the ice rink. I had just finished an adult ice hockey game at Eagles Ice Arena in Spokane, Washington. At the time I was stationed at Fairchild AFB and was flying with the Thirty-Sixth Rescue Flight.

My friend and I barely reached my car when my cell phone rang. I answered and it was our operations supervisor asking, "Have you had anything to drink? Are you available to fly search and rescue?"

The first question may sound strange, but for those of you who don't know, as a pilot in the USAF you are not allowed to have any alcohol within twelve hours of flying. We would call it a "twelve hours bottle to throttle," and I have seen many pilots watching the clock to know when they had to stop for the night. I quickly responded, "No. What are the details? I can go."

It was very exciting, something I had trained for. All those hours practicing, now I would have a chance to utilize the skills the Air Force had spent countless dollars on teaching me. I then asked, "Who will I be flying with?" I began to smile; the name I was given for my flight engineer was that very friend I had just walked out of the ice arena with.

He was still near his car. "Jake!" I yelled, "We have an SAR request." Now the military has so many acronyms (way before text shorthand), and for those who don't know, SAR stands for Search and Rescue.

Jake responded, "I'll see you at the unit." We both got in our vehicles and headed to our houses. I drove faster than I should have, reached my house, ran in, grabbed my flight suit and boots, then rushed back into the car.

I raced to the unit almost wanting to be pulled over for speeding. (I finally had a good excuse to speed.) Once there, I was met at the operations desk by our operations supervisor, who briefed me on what was happening. His intel told him there was a hiker who was injured during a day hike in the Cascades near Wenatchee. Apparently, he was a seasoned hiker who was hiking along a ridgeline, but he slipped and fell a thousand feet.

The call came in from an army soldier who had been hiking the same ridgeline with two of his friends. The three of them had watched the whole thing happen and had split up: two going to help the injured hiker and one running back down into town to call for help and provide information

Along with those details, he had given a general area of where to search for the three still on the mountain. Upon gathering all this information, I dispatched my copilot to preflight the aircraft and start running checklists. I sent Jake to preflight the hoist and gather the equipment needed for the rescue. We were also going to have a medic, and he was on his way in.

I began to plan: location, flight time, nearest hospitals, all the standard things you prep for. We all gathered our flight gear as necessary, including NVGs or night vision goggles, as it was full dark. I completed the flight planning and hurried to the hangar. There I found the aircraft outside, with Jake nearing completion and my copilot about to start the engines.

The medic gathered himself and began boarding the helicopter. I hopped into the right seat, donned my helmet, and began laying out the cockpit for the flight. My copilot started the engines and continued to run checklists.

We finished the engine run-up, and off we went. I calculated time en route and prepped the maps. As a crew we ran checklists, one for preparing the hoist for deployment, and one ensuring we knew where we were searching and how long we could stay overhead. It was at that point everything slowed down. It would take over forty-five minutes to reach the search area, and our adrenaline was starting to subside, so we started discussing what we might find when we got there.

I had been at Minot, North Dakota, for my previous assignment and had been performing security missions; this was my first true search and rescue. My actual first had been in the woods, at Cusick Washington and very simple, but that is a different story.

As we flew on, Jake shared some of his previous search and rescue missions. Of all the crew he had the most experience, having been on multiple SARs and working the rescue flight at Fairchild for over

four years. "He'll probably just have a twisted ankle," Jake said. "That's usually what happens. He probably just fell a few feet or something." We continued on and began to think this was going to be a normal, simple mission.

Soon we arrived at the Cascade Mountains, and I briefed the search area in greater detail. It was at this point that Jake spotted lights. We all looked to the south, and sure enough, about a thousand feet from the peak in a cirque was a flashing light. I turned the aircraft toward it.

Due to fuel beginning to get low, I started an approach to hover over the lights. I flew the aircraft down to the point where the light was coming from, and as we got closer, we spotted three people on a makeshift snow ledge.
 It turns out it was possible to fall a thousand feet and survive. Now, granted, it wasn't straight down, and the scene in *The Princess Bride* of dear Wesley falling down the hill flashed in my mind. Still, we didn't know how badly injured the survivor was. I continued my approach and slowed to a hover. It was at this point I realized this was not going to be "an easy mission."

If you have never used NVGs, the best way for me to describe it would be to imagine yourself looking at two tiny TV screens through cardboard tubes, then trying to drive through heavy traffic. You have no peripheral vision, so you learn to use other visual cues, one of which is used in flying by instruments only.

To remain level, you look at your attitude indicator, a spinning gyro that shows you how you are oriented to the earth. If the artificial horizon line is straight across left to right, you're in a level attitude. If it is on a slope, you're turning and, in the case of a hover, sliding sideways.

Well, looking through the NVGs at the mountain slope created a false horizon. This told my brain to move the helicopter right to level the aircraft. When I would do this, the aircraft would move away from the survivor. I had to listen to Jake, who was giving me my hover directions to position our helicopter over the survivor, enabling Jake to lower the medic down. I fought the urge to move left.

Once in position, I instructed my copilot to clear the left side of the aircraft and asked how much room we had from the blades to the mountain. "Five feet" was his response.

Oh boy, I thought. This was definitely not going to be an easy mission. Having a great crew and professional dialogue, as well as drawing on all my hours of training, I was able to hold the aircraft steady. Jake lowered the medic down to the shelf. Once he was on the ground, he detached from the hoist, and Jake raised the cable. We then flew away to allow the medic a less—we'll say hurricane—windy environment.

After taking off, we orbited to the north of the site and awaited word from the medic. Watching the fuel continue to decrease, I knew we didn't have a lot more time. I recalculated the fuel and realized we had about fifteen minutes until bingo fuel, a term used to describe a fuel state that would require you to abort the activity and begin flying to a refuel point.

It was at this time the medic was ready, and I proceeded inbound for the pickup. We came to a hover again. "There go his gloves," Jake said as we watched the rotor wash blow our medic's gloves down the mountain. He had taken them off to work on the survivor.

When we originally dropped off the medic, we had also lowered down a Stokes litter, which is a type of stretcher designed to be lifted up and down from the helicopter. Our medic had strapped the survivor into the litter, and we were hoisting him up.

As the Stokes litter got closer, Jake would verbally give us the play-by-play as was the standard practice of the day. This helped the pilots create a visual depiction in our minds as to how much longer we would be holding the hover. The Huey has no hover-hold button so it was all hands and feet. "Stokes halfway up," Jake stated; "Stokes at the skids," he continued; "Stokes coming in the cabin—wow, this dude's messed up!"

Not an easy mission as I initially thought.

Jake continued to pull in the survivor, strapped him down, and then proceeded to lower the hoist to pick up the medic. We accomplished this quickly as fuel was becoming scarce; we were actually at bingo fuel. Once

the medic was aboard, we proceeded to the predetermined hospital. At the hospital helipad, we were greeted by the medical staff, who unloaded the passenger, and then off we went to the nearest airport for fuel.

During the flight back to Fairchild, our medic described the survivor's injuries, which included broken ribs, broken legs, broken jaw and face bones, and lacerations. Later we found out he had multiple internal injuries too.

Nearing Fairchild, we were greeted by the sun rising. We had been up all night, but it was worth it. Our survivor made it and was doing well. So well, in fact, that months later he showed up at the rescue flight to say thanks and that he was about to go back out hiking again.

I hope you enjoyed this story, and I appreciate your attention as I relived the "glory days."

Thanks for reading.

G

ABOUT THE AUTHOR

Brent Golembiewski is a US Air Force veteran, retiring after Twenty-plus years of service.

He started his career as an enlisted troop, working as an electronic warfare technician. His first duty station was Shaw AFB, South Carolina, working on the AN/ALQ-182 jamming pod. It was here he picked up his nickname "G," which had begun as "G+11" due to his twelve-letter last name. It was later shortened to "G 11" then finally to just "G."

After being mentored by two of his training supervisors, Brent attended night school for one year and was then accepted to Bootstrap. He subsequently graduated from Embry-Riddle Aeronautical University with a bachelor's degree in professional aeronautics and a minor in safety.

Next, Brent completed Officer Training School (OTS) and was selected for pilot training at Columbus AFB, Mississippi, where he graduated Phase One of Undergraduate Pilot Training (UPT). He then headed to Fort Rucker, Alabama, for UPT Phase Two helicopter training. He graduated with his pilot wings and headed to Minot, North Dakota, to fly the UH-1N Huey helicopter.

Flying the mighty Huey has taken him many places, including Fairchild AFB, Washington; Baghdad, Iraq; Andrews AFB, Washington, DC; and F. E. Warren AFB, Wyoming.

Throughout his career, Brent continued his education, attending schools for safety investigation, mountain flying, instructor, and safety management. His USAF roles have included safety officer, flight commander, evaluator, flight instructor, and director of operations.

After retiring from the USAF, he began his company, Valkyrie, which provides aircraft charter operations. Brent and his wife, an active-duty Air Force helicopter pilot, have two boys, a giant Yetti, and a miniature ThunderCat.

I look forward to hearing from you! Check out my website for more stories and blogs

www.g11wingedhussar.com

or
email me at

g11wingedhussar@gmail.com

Low Flight

Oh, I've slipped the surly bonds of earth

And hovered out of ground effect on semi-rigid blades;

Earthward I've auto'ed and met the rising brush of non-paved terrain

And done a thousand things you would never care to

Skidded and dropped and flared

Low in the heat soaked roar.

Confined there, I've chased the earthbound traffic

And lost the race to insignificant headwinds;

Forward and up a little in ground effect

I've topped the General's hedge with drooping turns

Where never Skyhawk or even Phantom flew.

Shaking and pulling collective,

I've lumbered The low untresspassed halls of victor airways,

Put out my hand and touched a tree.

—Anonymous